52 Parenting Principles

"When we're raising children, every day can feel like a landmine of questions, concerns, and dilemmas. Dr. Miles Mettler is well aware of the common challenges that arise for parents—and he has great wisdom about the principles and approaches that make for solid, effective parenting."

Jim Daly, President, Focus on the Family

"During a time of parental confusion and anxiety, Dr. Miles offers sound, actionable, and encouraging advice to help parents. *52 Parenting Principles* is insightful, timely, and practical. Every parent should read this excellent book!"

Meg Meeker, MD, Best-selling Author of
Strong Fathers, Strong Daughters

"Have you noticed those EV charging stations springing up near you? Look at this insightful, helpful, encouraging book as a way to supercharge your parenting! Plug into each parenting concept, one here for each week. You'll find yourself better able to tackle the everyday hills, valleys and even potholes that come with parenting. Better yet, use these as weekly positive parenting charges with your spouse, or even a small group."

John Trent, Ph.D., President, StrongFamilies.com
and Author of *LifeMapping* and *The Blessing*

"Without wisdom, we're all in serious trouble. And with it, we—and our kids!—will flourish. This book is stacked with rock-solid wisdom, start to finish. What's more, it's easy to read, easily digestible, and perfect for discussion. So glad Miles wrote this."

Brant Hansen, Author of *Unoffendable, Blessed
Are the Misfits,* and *The Truth about Us*

"I love the concept of parenting your children in a way that you can have a wonderful relationship with them once they are adults. Multi-generational family impact is such an ancient and noble goal, and Miles has laid out a practical and action-oriented guide to help you parent with effective and long-term relationship in mind. This book will help you raise your kids the right way and is laid out in a way to build new actions and reactions inside your family. I highly recommend you get this book and start bringing out the best in yourself and your kids!"

Al Robertson, Pastor, Author, and Star of A&E's *Duck Dynasty*

"Raising children in today's world is hard. Raising my three boys, it was my goal to mentor and disciple them so they each had a strong foundation and so we would have a deep friendship through our entire lives. We have been through some beautiful highs and very challenging lows. Miles' book is invaluable, and I wish I'd had it twenty-five years ago! This book is what every parent needs. I'm so thankful Miles poured his life and heart into creating such a rich guide for parents today!"

John Ramstead, Author of *On Purpose with Purpose*, and Host of *Eternal Leadership Podcast*

"This book matters! It really matters—and it's written for the busy parent juggling time and emotional demands that come with raising today's children. Consuming and contemplating one short concise chapter a week is the ideal pace at which to glean the most out of it. The Action Steps alone are worth owning a copy. Dr. Miles Mettler cares deeply that parents succeed in being lifelong encouragers and cheerleaders for their kids. I share many strong and practical parenting books with people I meet—this one is now at the top of my list to give out."

Marlen Wells, Chaplain, Colorado Avalanche

"Parenting has never been harder. Miles Mettler's book is an invaluable resource that will help you raise healthy, godly kids. His '52 Principles' are comprehensive, practical, proven, and powerful."

David E. Clarke, Ph.D., Christian Psychologist, Podcaster, and Author of 15 Books, including *My Spouse Wants Out and I Didn't Want a Divorce, Now What?*

"Kids don't come with an instruction manual. In fact, the moment you leave the hospital to take your first baby home, it's a bit terrifying. Suddenly there is a baby in your arms with the same last name as yours and everyone is looking at you as if you are supposed to know what to do.

Parenting can feel like something that has just 'happened' to you, like you are being dragged behind something you don't understand and can't control. But what I most appreciate about Miles Mettler's *52 Parenting Principles* is how clearly he conveys that parenting is something you can do on purpose, something you can think through with a goal and plan in mind.

The chapters are short, quick reads. I recommend pacing your reading, in order to think and pray through the prompts and then apply them with wisdom. I appreciate his awareness of the uniqueness of each child and the need to tailor your parenting to their very different personalities. I also find valuable the way he describes parenting as something that needs to be coordinated between the team of father and mother.

52 Parenting Principles will help you identify your weak spots, the way all good coaching does. But, it gives very practical advice on how to overcome these weaknesses. In the end, I can think of no greater joy this side of heaven than to see your children grow up in faithfulness and love. This is a great tool to equip you in pursuing that end."

Ben Merkle, President, New Saint Andrews College

52
PARENTING
PRINCIPLES

HOW TO BRING OUT **THE BEST** IN YOUR KIDS

MILES METTLER, PH.D.

NEW YORK

LONDON • NASHVILLE • MELBOURNE • VANCOUVER

52 Parenting Principles

How to Bring Out the Best in Your Kids

Published in New York, New York, by Morgan James Publishing. Morgan James is a trademark of Morgan James, LLC. www.MorganJamesPublishing.com

Proudly distributed by Ingram Publisher Services.

Scripture quotations are taken from the *Daily Study Bible for Men*, New Living Translation (NLT), copyright ©1996, 2004, 2015 by Tyndale House Foundation. Used by permission of Tyndale House Publishers, Carol Stream, Illinois 60188. All rights reserved.

A FREE ebook edition is available for you or a friend with the purchase of this print book.

CLEARLY SIGN YOUR NAME ABOVE

Instructions to claim your free ebook edition:
1. Visit MorganJamesBOGO.com
2. Sign your name CLEARLY in the space above
3. Complete the form and submit a photo of this entire page
4. You or your friend can download the ebook to your preferred device

ISBN 9781631956867 paperback
ISBN 9781631956874 ebook
Library of Congress Control Number: 2021940783

Cover Design by:
Rachel Lopez
www.r2cdesign.com

Interior Design by:
Christopher Kirk
www.GFSstudio.com

Editorial:
Inspira Literary Solutions,
Gig Harbor, Washington

Morgan James is a proud partner of Habitat for Humanity Peninsula and Greater Williamsburg. Partners in building since 2006.

Get involved today! Visit MorganJamesPublishing.com/giving-back

This book is dedicated to:

. . . my parents, who, through their hard work, selflessness, and love, instilled values that serve and guide me to this day.

. . . my wife, who has been my steadfast, loving companion and compass in our journey together through life and raising four children.

. . . my four children, who fill my bucket while I admire their outstanding character and accomplishments, and who have made parenting a joy.

TABLE OF CONTENTS

Acknowledgments

No work of any size, small or large, is accomplished in isolation. In reflection, there are some key people who have contributed to this body of work being completed. In hindsight, where would I be without the patience of my typing teacher, Mrs. Bietz, when I was a senior in high school. Her class has proven to be one of the most beneficial in all my years of schooling and enabled thoughts to seamlessly escape from my head to paper.

In the beginning stages of drafting the book, Janet Blakely was the only person I told I was starting to write it. She willingly volunteered to review my first few chapters and eventually the entire book. Not only were her writing suggestions and edits invaluable, but she also offered continual encouragement and bolstered my confidence by convincing me there was value in my message that would benefit parents. Without her patience and persistence, the writing would not have continued or been completed. Everyone needs a Janet in their corner!

When the book was nearing its final stages, two additional special people offered to give the book a proofread and provide me with recommendations and changes. My mother-in-law, Linda Young, and my sister-in-law, Tara Young, offered edits and gentle but valuable suggestions, making the final work more readable and easy to understand.

When I signed up for a Zoom call for aspiring authors, it was with surprise and delight when another participant, Dennis Trittin, introduced himself. It so happened that I'd put a quote from Dennis in my book, which I mentioned when it was my turn to introduce myself. After the call, Dennis reached out via email, which led to an hour plus phone call. Dennis kindly walked me through what the publishing process would look like and patiently listened as I told him about my project. He then connected me with a professional editor with whom he'd worked, knowing that I needed assistance to get my book completed. His sincere desire to help was appreciated more than he'll ever know.

The editor that Dennis connected me with was Arlyn Lawrence, President of Inspira Literary Solutions. To sum it up—you wouldn't be reading this book without Arlyn's patience, guidance, and assistance. Arlyn was willing to take on my project after reading a small portion, and offered validation that what I had was unique and added value among the plethora of parenting literature in print. Step by step, she guided me to the finish line and was instrumental in a major publisher accepting my book for publication. It's not by accident that our paths crossed, and I couldn't have asked for a better-timed gift.

Along the way, there was a group of men who not only encouraged me but prayed for me during our weekly forums—my PFA Brothers: Michael Boerner, Greg Brooks, Brad Hawkins, Chris Kilcullen, Sean Kline, Drew Martin, Ben Merkle, Jerry Nichols, Paul Nichols, John Ramstead, and Tom Smith, whose support and willingness to share life experiences as we strive for the finish line was inspiring. I'm humbled to be with such a faithful group of men.

Then there were my children—Zachary, Maria, Matthew, and Anna—who provided me with a living laboratory to learn how to parent.

They allowed for my mess-ups and mistakes and offered love in exchange; that is unexplainable unless you are a father.

And of course there is Christy, the love of my life, who patiently waited and quietly supported bringing this book to life. Being a phenomenal mom, there is no one better with whom I can travel this parenting journey.

FOREWORD

Miles Mettler is a coach's coach, the kind of parenting coach I want to learn from. For decades, he has been distilling wisdom from Christian leaders. Now he has shared accessible parenting principles with a chapter for every week of the year.

I've known Miles for over twenty years. Out of the overflow of his experiences and his faith in Christ, he has written this book. *52 Parenting Principles: How to Bring Out the Best in Your Kids* is a valuable collection of principles (core truths) and patterns (repetition of principles). If practiced, it will provide any parent earnestly seeking to be better in their parenting role with a trustworthy compass (clear bearings and freedom to explore).

Consistently throughout this manual for parenting success, Miles reminds us that life—especially parenting—is hard, and God is good, and to not confuse the two. Miles does not pretend to have it figured out, and by his own admission is not always right, but anyone who knows Miles knows that he's always real. *52 Parenting Principles* is based on real knowledge and real experiences leading to real discoveries for parenting success.

What struck me in reading through each principle is that, without quoting tons of Scripture, these are core biblical truths in action. They reminded me of what God our Father is like and how, as His image bear-ers, we are to be like Him in all our relationships. From Miles' pen flows a belief in the Bible, and principles that reflect God's character.

Life is about relationships, is it not? If I were to re-title the book, it would be *52 Principles for Bringing Out the Best in Us!* And what's cool about that is out of the overflow of a deep and abiding relationship with Jesus, and living our best life with Him, will come parenting success.

I contend that *52 Parenting Principles* is a timeless treasure. With transparency and Christ-like humility, Miles writes as a man who's always learning and willing to fail forward and share what he's learned: profound and lifechanging truths—biblical principles—applied to parenting in new ways. Because I recognize Miles' careful thought and wise applica-tion of such accessible principles, I'm personally committing to walking through these principles one at a time (one a week) over the next year. I don't want to lose my MOJO!

Several years ago, I learned what it means to be truly coachable, read-ing the book by David Halberstam, *October 1964,* an ode to the World Series battle between the New York Yankees and Saint Louis Cardinals. Speaking about the Yankees' rookie star pitcher Mel Stottlemeyer, pitch-ing coach Billy Muffet declared, "He was a coach's dream, for he not only listened, but had the ability to turn what he learned into successful action." Miles Metter has proven himself coachable, and in *52 Principles* is encouraging us all to pursue the same goal, turning what we learn into successful action and living our best lives.

Are you coachable? If you are . . . this is a coach to learn from.

Tim Johnson
Regional Director
Fellowship of Christian Athletes

INTRODUCTION

After the birth of our third child, I was wishing for some sort of instruction book to provide answers and solutions for my mounting list of parenting questions. So, I went looking for help—primarily buying books and pouring through their content. The authors, many highly qualified professionals, offered sound theory and rationale for what to do and what not to do.

Some books were written specifically for boys and others for girls. We had both, so naturally we tried to decipher what unique approaches to use for our two sons versus our two daughters as they grew and matured. There were those that hinted at instant results if we followed the methods they outlined. Did everything we tried work? No, but perhaps we didn't fully understand or implement the suggestions properly.

I imagine most parents go through this process, precariously balancing between their aspirations and their actual experience in parenting. What kind of father or mother do *you* aspire to be? I don't know any parents who love their kids and simultaneously desire to be bad at parenting. But sometimes, as parents, my wife Christy and I would face problems that made our parenting skills seem insufficient. When that happened, I'd find myself asking, "What's missing?"

Children don't come with an owner's manual. In some respects, they really can't. All kids are different. If there were a parenting "owner's manual," wouldn't we diligently try to follow the instructions, applying the methods to each child, striving to get the desired outcome . . . the "perfect" child!? I figured there must be some sort of plan we could follow.

And it wasn't just me. Being involved in the health and fitness profession, I worked closely with other adults and often heard not only about their health concerns, but also about problems they were having with their children. Some had young children, while others had children who were grown and no longer living at home. But, one thing they all had in common was that, like me, they were looking for answers.

In addition to common issues parents face, one consistent, overriding concern parents shared with me was that the relationship they had with their children was not healthy. Somewhere along the journey, seemingly irreparable damage was done and hope of restoration was lost. My heart often broke hearing stories of fragmented families and strained relationships.

In addition to rereading the parenting books I had on my shelf, I decided to review some of the educational material I had studied years earlier in pursuit of my doctorate in exercise and wellness. Some of the pieces started to coalesce. My studies had been heavily steeped in personal responsibility and behavior change. In reviewing the information, I began to see how these principles could be applied to more than health and fitness.

It was fascinating to find out, whether related to health or parenting, that our ingrained habits often produce the opposite effect of what we want. I'd always suspected our upbringing, and the environment in which we were immersed growing up, influenced our behavior as adults. But I never appreciated the degree to which that was true. What makes it even more challenging is when each parent has a distinctly different upbringing.

The behaviors we grew up experiencing directly impact how we parent . . . unless we learn otherwise. No wonder I'd encountered so many parents struggling to develop or maintain a healthy relationship with their children.

Being a parent is the hardest and most challenging responsibility you'll encounter. That's why being an intentional parent is worth the effort. Parenting takes enormous energy, regardless of whether or not you take time to learn a better way. In fact, by investing time to learn new methods and ways of connecting with your children, you'll most likely find you're simultaneously conserving energy and storing up positive memories. And, not to understate it, but do you recognize that what you do as a parent now not only impacts your children, but will influence your grandchildren through the parenting they receive, as well?

This book is about how to build relationships with your children as you parent. You are seeking to develop and maintain a healthy relationship now so you can be a positive force in their life throughout adulthood. A word of caution: you can overvalue the relationship so much that you fail to do your job as a parent and neglect to teach them how to be accountable for their actions and behavior. When children sense this is happening, they will assume a false sense of power, which ironically leads to insecurity and ultimately damages your relationship.

So, it isn't all roses. Love requires and demands hard choices from parents who have the best interests of their children in mind, even if the children don't seem to appreciate it in the moment. As a result, loving your children in a healthy manner may initially appear to damage your relationship, but the mature parent knows that the feeling is only temporary.

The intent for this book is to provide relatively concise, practical parenting strategies with a little insight to add context. The information is presented as 52 principles, some with closely related concepts and lessons. It's designed for you to read and begin applying one principle per week over the course of a year. You can work your way through the book sequentially or pick and choose different sections week to week.

Or, you may want to read the entire book first and then decide where to begin. You may work on some principles for only a day, but probably spend weeks on others. There is no ideal timeline so long as you are learning and applying the concepts along the way. Use it as a guide and keep track of your progress. And, with a little creativity, you can adapt most all of the principles to suit kids of any age.

The time it takes to strengthen, renew, or maybe even restore your relationship with your children is worth whatever investment you are willing to make. I hope this practical guide will be your companion along the way as you discover and apply *52 Parenting Principles*!

THE PRINCIPLES

OWN THE PROBLEM

Most of us like to solve problems and make things better. It's our nature. When we know a family member or friend is having difficulties, our mind will instinctively seek solutions in an effort to help. But, what if I'm the one with the problem? Personally, I try to figure most things out for myself. For good or bad, seldom do I bring others into the picture to help me.

My nature is to look outward for solutions rather than inward. Why would I instinctively think that *I'd* be the cause of problems I was having, especially with my kids? It was always easy to focus on what our *kids* needed to do differently and how they need to change. I'm older, wiser, and have more experience, right? How could I be the cause of their behavior problems?

As I mentioned in the introduction, my previous studies and research related to behavior change led to insights that would make a difference in my parenting, as well. It finally clicked! One day I realized that *I* would have to change first before I'd begin to see changes in our children. As you probably have experienced, breakthroughs often happen when we're in the darkest places. I was humbled when the light finally came on and I realized far too often that I was at fault.

Comprehending that we need to change first may be one of the hardest and most challenging concepts we have to embrace when it comes to raising children. This notion was reinforced when I read Dr. Kevin Lehman's book, *Have a New Kid by Friday*. He clearly conveyed the concept that if we don't like how things are between our kids and us, we may need to change first! However, admitting the conflicts I encountered with my children were because of what I was doing wasn't an easy pill to swallow.

When we think the children are the problem and need to change, that attitude is reflected in how we relate to them. They can sense our judgmental attitude, and when they do, those feelings actually inhibit them from changing. What we're really doing when we display that mindset is sending messages to our kids that they aren't okay as they are, so they need to be fixed. As you can imagine, however, no one likes to feel like they're a problem in need of fixing, especially our children.

Since we can never directly change other people, including our kids, our attention needs to be on what we can control. And, as was referenced, the only thing we can change is ourselves. (If you're control-oriented, this concept may leave you feeling very uneasy.) American business philosopher Jim Rohn said, "You must take personal responsibility. You cannot change the circumstances, the seasons, or the wind, but you can change yourself."

So where do we begin? The initial step toward making a breakthrough is to accept 100 percent responsibility. In his book, *The Success Principles*, author Jack Canfield wrote, "If you want to be successful, you have to take 100 percent responsibility for everything that you experience in your life. This includes the level of your achievement, the results you produce, the quality of your relationships, the state of your health and physical fitness, your income, your debts, your feeling—everything." He went on to say, "…most of us have been conditioned to blame something outside of ourselves for the parts of our life we don't like . . . we never want to look where the real problem is—ourselves."

We are much better served by taking ownership of the problem, and not look to place responsibility elsewhere. To establish positive relationships with our children, blaming our children or seeing them as the problem cannot be part of the solution. Looking primarily at what the kids need to do differently (blaming), means we're looking outward rather than inward. In other words, our emphasis on how we're approaching our kids implies that they are always at fault, instead of being on what and how we can improve. It's unlikely that any permanent change for the better will occur with that approach!

Have you ever been on the receiving end of blame? Growing up as the youngest of five boys, I have—and it's one of the worst feelings to experience. However, it's one thing being blamed by your siblings, but when it comes from a parent the hurt is much deeper.

One of the fundamental problems with blame is that our orientation is on the past and not the future. I'll discuss that in more detail later on in the book. In that state, we're likely to think and say things to our kids like, "You should have," or, "How come you did that," or "Why didn't you _____?" Comments like those highlight that we think *they* are the cause of the problem.

However, we're much better served by first zeroing in on what we can do differently and how we can change, which will lead to better and more productive outcomes. Motivational speaker Wayne Dyer is quoted as saying, "All blame is a waste of time. No matter how much fault you find with another, and regardless of how much you blame him, it will not change you."

A simple way to initiate this change is to ask yourself questions like, "How can I show up differently?" and "How can I respond in a better manner?" The key to achieving better results is to ask ourselves better questions, questions that will cause us to focus on ourselves and improvements we can make.

Our children need to know we are for them! If they feel like we only see them as a problem to be fixed, then their sense of self will be stifled, and they'll develop a load of self-doubt. Is that what you want? I know I don't.

Please don't be confused by what I'm saying. Our children are still responsible for their behavior. And you are responsible for yours. But when I step back and am willing to accept that the relationship problems I am having (or want to avoid) may stem from my attitude, words, and actions, it allows me to see my children from a different perspective.

It took several weeks of intentionally focusing on my attitude and willingness to accept 100 percent responsibility before it really impacted how I was relating to our kids. When they realized that I was accepting responsibility by working on my own behavior, our children reciprocated by taking more ownership of their choices, as well. Ironically, this approach enhanced my relationship with them and led to more of the positive changes I'd been seeking.

Reflection and Discussion Questions:

1. What are recurring situations in which you only notice what your children are doing wrong?
2. What is the ideal outcome you're looking to achieve with your child(ren)?

Action Steps:

1. Have a heart-to-heart talk with yourself, asking yourself, *Am I accepting 100 percent responsibility related to the parenting challenges I'm having with my children?*
2. Consider praying this prayer each morning, before you start your day: "Lord, I'm responsible for how I talk to my children and for what I say. Please give me the grace and patience I need. Help my words be edifying to You and to them. Amen."

CRAFT A FAMILY VISION STATEMENT

Articulating a well-defined vision is commonplace for leaders in most organizations and businesses, but seldom heard of for families. The reason a business executive sets a clear vision is because a vision statement moves people in a positive direction, so the organization accomplishes more, and everyone involved can share in the experience.

In their thought-provoking book, *The 12-Week Year*, Moran and Lennington said, "The secret to living your life to its potential is to value the important stuff above your own comfort. Therefore, the critical first step to executing well is to create and maintain a compelling vision of the future . . . Think about what you truly want to achieve. What legacy do you want to create? What do you want for yourself and for your family?" As they state, "Vision is the starting point of all high performance . . . If you find you're lacking passion in either your business or in a relationship, it's not a crisis of passion; it's a crisis of vision."

The business world doesn't hold a patent on vision statements. An appropriately crafted vision can also coalesce families around a picture of what their future can look like. A family vision statement can help motivate family members and bring context to rules and guidelines, so the vision can become a reality.

I'm guessing you probably don't have a vision statement written out for your family. If you do, way to go! You've done something most parents haven't even considered. It took us until our youngest child was born to begin the process. Or, maybe you've thought about the vision you have for your family, but haven't taken time to put it down on paper. If so, well done; you're part of the way there!

But, if you're like most parents, you've most likely never even thought about creating one or just don't know how or where to start. We hadn't really either. I'd read many books on leadership and most all of them included some mention of "setting the vision." But it had never dawned on me that I should do it for my family! Then, one day I thought, *If it's important for business leaders to do it for their organization, it's probably a good idea for us to do it for our family as well.* And that's how it started. Had we not taken the time and put in the effort to create a vision statement for our family, Christy and I would have missed an important opportunity for leaving an indelible mark and securing our family legacy.

I understand creating a vision statement can be a challenging exercise for many parents. Some are worried they may leave something out, making it feel incomplete. Others fear it's too grandiose of an exercise to accomplish, or don't really believe it will make a difference.

The vision statement is only a few paragraphs put on paper, describing the best hopes and aspirations we have for our family. In our vision statement, Christy and I included the type of environment we were striving to develop, the depth of relationships we wanted to experience, and the impact we felt we could have as a family unit. It was a collective document outlining, in large part, what overall behaviors would be required of our individual family members in order to fulfill the vision as it was stated.

Depending upon the age of the children, crafting a vision statement can be a family project, or each spouse can write up his or her own version. Working together, the couple can then compile their documents into one final vision statement to share with the family.

When writing your own vision statement, be sure to allow ample, uninterrupted time to complete the initial draft. The first time through, the main goal is to get something down on paper (or on the screen, if you're doing it electronically). There will be time after the initial draft is created for you to go back through and make edits, modifications, and additions as you see fit. Just getting it written out the first time will feel like an accomplishment!

Once your vision statement is crafted, schedule a time for a family gathering to read your new vision out loud for everyone to hear. It'll be beneficial to have prepared hard copies to hand out to all family members after you've read it. Even if you have children too young to read, hand them their own personal copy with their name on it, so they feel special and included. Provide time for discussions to answer questions regarding the new direction your family is headed. It may be obvious, but just as professional vision statements are written to inspire and give clarity to why the organization's work is important, your words should also serve to inspire and provide an uplifting message with clarity.

Like all vision statements, after it's created, the real value is to make it a living and breathing part of family life. As you can probably guess, putting it in a file drawer or hanging it on the wall won't bring it alive nor will it have the impact it was designed to have without regularly reviewing it as a family, and together as a couple. It'll be fun to discuss the progress your family is seeing toward making the vision becoming a reality. Use the reflection and discussion questions as an opportunity to create short-term action plans or goals for the family, or each individual, to follow in order to stay on track.

We become what we focus on. The vision statement provides focus. As Christy and I learned, without having a vision statement, our family had no tangible goals to pursue as a unified body, and life was just happening.

As we've all heard too often, the time we have with our children is short and it goes fast. Perhaps you have older kids and are thinking you've lost your opportunity or it's too late to create a vision statement. Think again. Unless they're out of the house and you have no contact with them, it's not too late.

Novelist Henry James said, "It's time to start living the life you've imagined." That's what a vision statement will help you do . . . imagine the life you'd like to live. I know it may seem daunting, but take action! Schedule time to create yours before another week goes by. Over time you'll most likely want to tweak your statement, but once it's in place, you and your family will never live another day without vision.

Reflection and Discussion Questions:

1. How might a family vision statement help your family and how do you feel about creating one?
2. What is stopping you from moving forward to create a vision statement, and what do you need to do to get started?

Action Steps:

1. Schedule a half day of uninterrupted time to start crafting your vision statement. Be flexible and allow more time, if needed.
2. Share it with the family to get some feedback, then rework, edit, and finalize the vision statement. Print and present copies to all family members and celebrate the new direction for your family.

Be Intentional at Home

f I were to ask you to describe your home environment, what would you say? How would you describe it? Would your description make me laugh . . . or cry? If yours is like most households, it's probably a mixed bag of tension and tears, laughter and joy, commotion and chaos, and anger and frustration.

What if I told you that you're able to control what happens in your home more than you realize? As parents, we're responsible for creating the home life we want our family members to experience. We can consider it a major part of our leadership role. So, what's the environment you want to cultivate in your home? Being intentional about the environment we want to create maybe isn't something most moms or dads have even thought about. I know for several years, we didn't. But, if we don't want to live in regret, being intentional about what we want our children to experience at home is a great place to start.

Keep in mind, your home environment has already been created and is in place. The question is: is it the environment you and your children desire, or can you envision something better?

In our hearts, we long to have the best possible relationship with our children and want to see them become their best selves. When we're working toward that goal, being intentional about the environment we want to create will take precedence. To help the process, I encourage you to begin thinking about the outcome you'd like to achieve. As Stephen R. Covey famously recommends, "Begin with the end in mind."

Imagine, if things stay as they are in your home, and twenty years from now your children are reminiscing about what it was like growing up in your home, what do you think they'll say? What is it you hope they will say? How do you want them to remember their years under your roof? Is the home environment you're currently creating going to elicit those memories?

Being intentional about what our family will experience in our home can begin by strategically laying out a list, which identifies the best image we have for our household. Some traits to include are references to the tenor, the atmosphere, and the vibe we want. We can ask ourselves questions like, "What do we want our household to be famous for?" And, "When someone visits and spends a few days in our home, what will they experience by observing and seeing how we interact with our kids . . . and our children with us?"

When I initially created mine, I kept the list to myself and reread it daily in order to keep it top of mind. Then I stealthily began implementing it by preparing myself for how I was going to show up when I got home from work. There were also some specific behaviors I had to tackle, including becoming more aware of my non-verbal signals and gestures and thinking more before I spoke to make sure I was coming across as intended.

One fundamental change I made when our kids were young was to say to them, "I love you." That one action has made the most significant difference over anything I've done as a father. This may or may not be a big deal for you, but for me, it was a game changer, both for me and our kids. Not only did I tell them I loved them, but I also started giving them hugs—often, and without cause! Part of the reason it was a big deal for me is because I don't ever recall my dad telling me verbally that he loved me. Even though I know he did, saying the words just wasn't something that he did. It wasn't part of our home environment. So, one day I had a moment of clarity and inspiration to say the words and show the affection by hugging. To this day, our oldest is in his twenties, and telling him I love him and hugging is common practice . . . all because I became intentional about it when he was about five years old.

The key is to be continually mindful of these changes, so they become a consistent part of your behavior. The start of your transformation may be subtle but, regardless, stay committed to the process. When I felt the time was right, I shared my list of intentional changes with everyone in our family. I did so because I wanted them to know the heart I had for our family and to see that I was willing to work on creating an environment in which they could thrive.

There's power behind being intentional. Involving your kids to help you see changes you can make, as appropriate, will benefit them the rest of their lives, as well. When they're older, they'll recall how you modeled behaviors they appreciated and made them feel loved. Ideally, it'll be something they adopt with their families and become a family trademark that started with you!

Reflection and Discussion Questions:

1. Twenty years from now, when your kids are reminiscing about what it was like growing up in your home, what do you want them to say?

2. What was your home environment like while you were growing up? How much is that influencing you today? Is it mostly positive, or negative?

ACTION STEPS:

1. Identify one change you can make that would make the biggest difference to improve your home environment and initiate that change today.

2. Get input from your children. Ask them for one improvement they'd like to see in your home.

PRINCIPLE 4

ASK FOR FEEDBACK

enerally speaking, I was never one to ask for help if I encountered
problems. That tendency also played out in how I received feedback, or what some may call "advice." Advice was something I gave
out . . . I didn't need to receive it! Without undergoing psychoanalysis,
I'm guessing it's because I didn't want to feel like I was at fault, or that
something was wrong with me. Or, perhaps I just didn't want to admit
I might be saying or doing the wrong things. So, I'd usually go into
defensive mode anytime I received criticism or feedback, even if it was
in my best interest.

But, eventually I realized that if I want to improve, I'm much better
off accepting feedback as my friend, and not view it as if I've failed. A
friend is someone who comes to your aid when you're in need of help.
Feedback can be like that friend who will tell you the truth, even if it's
not what you want to hear. So, learning to adopt a mindset that there's no
such thing as failure, only feedback, is a healthy perspective and essential
for personal and professional growth.

As parents, when we not only *welcome* feedback but we also *ask
for it,* and are open to change, it models a critical attribute that will be

fundamental for our kids' future success. When they watch us seek and solicit ways to improve, it will help prepare them for life. If they learn how to welcome and accept feedback at an early age, they'll be able to demonstrate unusual maturity when they receive it from teachers in school, and from managers or customers when they enter the workforce, which will give them a leg up. So, we can be assured that when we're more open to change and grow, it prompts our children to be more accepting of feedback, as well. That's worth whatever price it takes to put our ego in check!

A unique type of feedback, which I call Transformation Feedback, is much more effective in creating sustainable change than traditional feedback. This type of feedback isn't fixated on what a person does wrong. Instead, the emphasis is on what the person can do in the future—suggestions for improvement. Traditional feedback is a review of what's happened in the past. Too often, people view feedback as criticism or an attack on their character and immediately become defensive. And, frequently the person providing the feedback can come across as negative and judgmental, even if that's not the intent.

But, asking our children questions like, "What can I do to be a better dad?" or, "How can I be more supportive?" puts the focus on what we can do moving forward, not on the mistakes we've made in the past. Questions of this nature give us something to focus on as parents, not something to defend or feel bad about. Plus, this strategy provides our kids with a voice and an opportunity to contribute directly to our improvement.

If you're brave enough to try this, it's important to be consistent in the process and not just give it lip service. Genuinely seek suggestions and act on the recommendations, and then ask for follow up on how you're doing. Of course, you still have to discriminate and use your best judgment with the feedback you're receiving. But, research indicates regular accountability, which is what feedback provides, from someone we trust can significantly enhance our ability to experience sustainable change.

Try this method with your spouse as well. Do you have people you lead in the workplace? Try Transformation Feedback with them. You might be surprised how quickly it can transform you and those you lead, including your children.

Reflection and Discussion Questions:

1. When you give feedback, is it highlighting what your children did wrong, or suggesting improvements moving forward?
2. After reading this principle, what do you think you need to change about the way you provide or respond to feedback?

Action Steps:

1. Let your kids know that you're working to become a better parent and would like their help. Pick a couple of questions— like those above—and ask your kids for their thoughts.
2. In a couple of weeks, follow up and engage them in a discussion about how they think you're doing.

PRINCIPLE 5

'FeSS UP WHeN YOU MeSS UP

Relatively speaking, we know a lot and have much more experience than our children. But, we're not perfect. Are we? You and I make mistakes. I inevitably make wrong choices at work, at home, and in how I parent. Not sure how you stack up in the mistake department? Just ask your children, if you dare!

However, making mistakes isn't what really damages our relationship with our children. Our relationship is impaired when we know we make a mistake but brush over it or fail to recognize and admit we are in error. Basically, our pride gets in the way, for one thing. Additionally, when they admit failure or mistakes, parents are likely to feel as if they're conveying weakness or diminishing their position of authority. Ironically, the opposite is true.

Oddly, when we don't worry about being right, but are willing to 'fess up and admit we're wrong, it helps us grow in stature in the eyes of our children (and our spouse). As you know, children model what they see. When your children see you 'fess up when you mess up, they are much more likely to do the same.

So, there is a better way, if you're interested in trying a different and much more effective communication strategy with your children when you have messed up. Here's what I call the 4-A method to follow when you find yourself in a situation where you have made a mistake. Follow these four steps to see what a difference it can make:

1. Acknowledge you made a mistake. *(I was wrong for criticizing you.)*
2. Apologize. *(I'm sorry for doing that.)*
3. Ask for forgiveness. *(Please forgive me.)*
4. Affirm the relationship. *(I love you.)*

That's it.

However, as simple as that sounds, it's VERY CRITICAL to never ruin an apology with an excuse. Our human nature is to defend or justify our actions. But to do so ruins the whole apology. Never at any point in the 4-A sequence or immediately afterward, offer an excuse or reason.

For example, we naturally want to explain why we yelled or were short or didn't listen. So, we'll make excuses and say things like, "I was tired," or "I was busy," or "I was running late." But it doesn't matter.

That's because making any type of excuse does two things. First, it ruins the apology and makes it seem insincere. Second, it's the exact opposite of the behavior we're trying to model. We're looking to instill the character quality of taking 100 percent responsibility for our actions . . . no excuses. If we make excuses, we're not setting a very good example!

I hope you will try the 4-A method. It may take some time, but with practice you'll become a master and, ironically, find you need to apologize much less often. Be aware, the reaction you get the first few times you do it may surprise you!

Reflection and Discussion Questions:

1. If/when you apologize now, do you find yourself justifying, making excuses, or giving a reason why you did what you did?

2. After you use the 4-A method, observe the reaction from your children. What do you notice?

ACTION STEPS:

1. Rehearse the 4-A method in your mind and visualize yourself using it with your children.
2. Pick something that happened recently you could apologize for and use the 4-A method.

PRINCIPLE 6

PLANT GOOD SEEDS

Modeling is very important. We all assess people more by what we see them do than by what they say. In other words, our actions often speak louder than our words, no matter how forcefully we may talk.

Our children are no different in how they learn. No matter what we say, they'll learn the most and model most closely what they see in us. So, we want to be acutely aware of the qualities and behaviors we're displaying and the actions we're taking on a daily basis.

For example, Christy and I are runners. Both of us have been running for most of our lives. It's what our children have seen us do since they were born. Now all four children are runners, too. They have talent, and so do a lot of other kids. But talent doesn't account for the initiative they take when they call their friends to meet them at the track no matter what the weather conditions. You see, they have seen us suit up and head out the door, regardless of the weather, for as long as they can remember. Thankfully, now they're following suit.

So, how can we be diligent about instilling qualities we believe are important in our children (or in people we lead)? One worthwhile exercise to get started is to identify the characteristics and qualities we'd most like our kids to develop and display.

We simply have to ask ourselves this question, "What are some of the most important characteristics and qualities I'd like _____ _____(names of our children) to have?"

STOP HERE AND DO THIS EXERCISE BEFORE YOU MOVE ON.

What does your list look like? Some of the common qualities parents identify include:

- honesty
- compassion
- truthfulness
- kindness
- patience
- love/loving
- gentleness
- happiness
- joy
- competence
- diligence
- persistence
- resilience
- self-confidence
- thankfulness
- gratitude
- graciousness
- generosity
- good listening
- respectfulness
- enthusiasm

- passion
- peacefulness
- positivity
- optimism
- more???

I know it might seem difficult, but if you have more than five traits listed, and most likely you will, take a minute and identify your top five choices—the order doesn't matter at this point. Now here's the surprise . . . and moment of truth. As you review your top five, ask yourself, "How well do I match, mimic, and model the characteristic listed—my top five?"

Doing this exercise will reveal a meaningful insight: You may not have realized it, but chances are that the top qualities you chose for your children are also the most important traits you aspire for yourself, even if you don't currently model those behaviors. So, since you're now more aware of what qualities you personally value, you can be more intentional about displaying those behaviors day in and day out.

If you're curious about how this may tie into Scripture, one of God's fundamental laws is of planting and harvesting. Galatians 6:7 states, "You will always reap what you sow." That principle applies to every area of life, including parenting. The law states we first give away (plant) whatever we want more of.

In all areas of life, it's best to be intentional about the seeds we're sowing. For example, to make it personal, if compassion is on your list, do your children see you being compassionate? If you have patience on your list, do you model patience for your children? I think you get the picture.

The concept is quite simple. If we want our children to be compassionate, they should see compassion in us—we want to sow seeds of compassion. It would be disingenuous to expect our children to produce something we're not sowing. If we tell our kids to be kind, but we're not, we lose credibility and authority in their eyes.

When we tell them to be positive, but they hear us complain when something goes wrong, what message does that send? How will they respond when life deals them a bad hand? Most likely, they'll emulate how they've seen us behave.

We want what's best for our children. And the qualities and characteristics they develop growing up will fundamentally shape their ability to be effective and successful in living out God's call for their lives. Such a life will require developing and growing in Christlike character.

In case you're wondering, according to 2 Corinthians, here are the characteristics Christ displayed: love, service, sacrifice, kindness, gentleness, boldness, dependability, compassion, empathy, courage, tenderheartedness, graciousness, and generosity.

Whether a Christ-follower or not, everyone probably desires qualities such as these for their children. If we can help them develop those traits, they'll be well positioned to live a great life with meaning and purpose. The best way we can help is to live them ourselves . . . planting as many seeds as we can.

REFLECTION AND DISCUSSION QUESTIONS:

1. What qualities (good and bad) did you your parents model for you when you were growing up?
2. Is there anything holding you back from modeling the qualities you identified in your own list?

ACTION STEPS:

1. Make a list of the most important characteristics and qualities you'd like your children to have.
2. Narrow the list to the top five. This week, be intentional about modeling each of those characteristics.

START FOCUSING ON THE POSITIVE

"The mind left unattended will drift toward the negative." I heard that statement a long time ago; it stuck in my mind and continues to prove true today. As much as I don't like it, it's our human nature. The New Testament Scriptures give us some clues about that and, most likely, it's why we're instructed in Philippians 4:8 to focus on what is true and admirable and holy. And it's also probably why Paul encourages us in Romans 12:2 not to be conformed to the world, but to be transformed by the renewing of our mind. If we're Christ-followers, we have the power of the Holy Spirit helping to shape our thoughts.

This "proclivity for negativity" can lead us to only (or mostly) see what our children are doing *wrong*. Our intentions may be worthy—after all, we want what's best for them, right? However, our default mode can be primarily to point out what they're doing wrong or need to do better. If we're not careful, this negative attitude toward our children can easily become a habit.

To help combat an inclination to focus on the negative, I've found it helpful to write down what it is I admire about our children. If you have more than one child, no doubt you've observed at various times their uniqueness, as well as their similarities. Probably when you're not even expecting it, your kids will do something that catches your attention and causes you to pause and reflect . . . with admiration.

I remember one afternoon, during a break in the school calendar, I noticed my daughter was in her room all afternoon. Not knowing what she was doing, I decided to check and ask her what she was up to. The answer was one of those moments that caused me to pause and reflect and express my admiration. She had found out a boy in her class had been quarantined at home for three months. So, thinking about how it must feel to be isolated from your peers for so long, she organized a letter-writing campaign with her friends. Since they weren't all able to get their letters to her in person, she had them text or email what they wanted to say, and then she painstakingly transcribed every single letter by hand.

I had the privilege of driving her to the boy's home (beaming with pride) as she secretly delivered the pile of handwritten notes to his front door. To this day, I am still struck by the thoughtfulness and care she displayed in not only organizing the whole letter drive, but in volunteering to write all the letters herself so the boy could have a physical reminder of his classmates.

What are the special qualities and characteristics you've observed in *your* children? What have you identified that's unique about them? What are some of the gifts and talents they possess?

Simply because I've posed these questions, you're more likely to start focusing on the positive traits your children display. So, in the coming days, it'll be important to take time and make note of what you're observing. Making a simple list will be good a start, but you may find it more helpful to write your answers out in paragraph form. Write as if you're writing to each child. Then, at least once a week, take time to read what you've written as a reminder, so it stays fresh in your mind. I believe your thinking can be transformed over time and you'll have renewed appreciation for each of your children.

Since we now know that what we focus on (think about) grows, centering on their positive qualities makes it more probable we'll notice and acknowledge those traits on a consistent basis moving forward. However, if we pay primary attention or focus on what our children do wrong, then that's what we'll observe and point out. I think it's pretty obvious which is the better and more desirous approach.

By taking time to identify and do the above exercise—to know what it is we admire about our children, even in times when they make bad choices—we'll be more apt to respond in a manner more pleasing and productive for everyone.

REFLECTION AND DISCUSSION QUESTIONS:

1. How would you describe yourself . . . are you "naturally" positive or more negative? How would your spouse or friends describe you?
2. Reminisce and describe times your recall when your children did something you admired. Why did it stick out to you and how did it make you feel?

ACTION STEPS:

1. Make a list of what you admire about each of your children. Pick their top three qualities, in your opinion.
2. In paragraph form for each of the top three characteristics, write out the quality you've observed, when you've observed it, and why it's important to you. When you notice those traits being exhibited in your children, be intentional about pointing them out.

NAVIGATE THE TECHNOLOGY TRAP

The seemingly sudden explosion of personal technology gadgets that have emerged in recent years has ushered in a complex array of new devices for us to manage. Never in our lifetime have we had state-of-the-art technology at our fingertips, continually distracting us through seductive sounds and stimulating visuals. And, parents now have to debate about what is an appropriate age to get their teenager (or younger) a smartphone! In order for us to navigate through the age of technology traps, I'm advocating for families to reevaluate their routines in order to reconnect at home.

Daily occurrences remind us that families are busier than ever. While at a coffee shop, I overheard two retired men lamenting about their grown children not attending church because they say they're too busy at this time in their lives. Their concern was not only for their kids, but that their grandchildren would be missing out on a key time in their lives to learn about and grow in their faith . . . all because their parents were "too busy."

I'm not casting blame, as I'm sure we can all relate to the many times we've gone to bed without everything done on our to-do list. But that in itself is interesting, because ideally all our smart technology is meant to improve productivity and communication in order to make our lives easier, less stressed, and less busy, so we (supposedly) have time for what and who we most value. Would you agree that something doesn't seem to be working right?

It's pretty easy to see that our adoption and utilization of cell phones and other devices has affected most every area of our life. For example, conversations around the dinner table—on the rare occasion when families eat together—are commonly interrupted by someone being drawn to their device. Too often parents and/or children have their phone positioned next to their plate . . . the cell phone has become part of the new table setting. Even if I don't intend to use my phone, if it's within an arm's reach, there's an unconscious draw preventing me from being fully engaged in conversation. In addition, in many homes, the TV is also on during the meal, which creates further distraction and inhibits meaningful conversation and enjoyment. And who can get through a meal without asking "Alexa" a question or two?

Ironically, technology promises to connect people in ways never previously imagined. But, paradoxically, combined with our busy lifestyles, we've never been more disconnected from those who mean the most to us. The dopamine response we get when the device dings or beeps or rings causes us to divert our attention immediately, regardless of what we're doing, even in the middle of conversations. But, it doesn't have to be that way. The technology we possess is ours to also manage—not the other way around.

When Christy and I started to realize our family was being impacted, the first exercise we collectively did was to identify how we were being negatively affected by all aspects of technology, especially our cell phones. Then we discussed why it was important to make changes. The next step was to get everyone on the same page, or to at least understand our rationale for the strategies we wanted to implement to eliminate distractions and improve communication.

To give you some ideas, just a couple of the approaches we agreed to include no phones at the dinner table and no looking at their phone or any device when talking to each other. It was nothing complicated to start, but in some cases, it was not easy, either. What we found as a result was that our conversations improved, conflict was reduced, we felt more connected, and we achieved common ground for communicating at home.

As the cell phone gets smarter and smarter, our job is to recognize the positive and negative impact on our families and change what's not working, so our families can thrive even in the midst of the technology explosion. Technology is here to stay and will be a part of our life we need to learn to navigate. We can use it to enhance our quality of life, or we can allow it to disrupt and distract from what's really important. The choice is ours.

Reflection and Discussion Questions:

1. How have you noticed technology interrupting your family life?
2. What three changes can your family make to improve communication and reduce distraction?

Action Steps:

1. Hold a family meeting and get everyone's input. Chart a new course by setting up agreed-upon guidelines to help manage the technology in your home.
2. Approximately one month after implementation, review with your family what changes they are noticing (good and bad) and make any additional changes or modifications to continue on this path.

LISTEN WITH L.O.V.E.

I f you have a dog in your home, and it's like ours, have you noticed how it runs to the door to greet you when you come home? I know for our dog, if I stop, even for 10 seconds, and get down and greet her and give her a good rub, she's happy and runs off. But if I walk past her or just tap her on the head, she'll continually follow me until she's been loved and acknowledged. Think about what's happening there: initial acknowledgement, undivided attention, physical affection, and words of affirmation. With that kind of interaction, her needs are met, and she trots off with a happy heart.

At one point, I noticed that applying parallel logic to our children seemed odd, but it was effective. Interestingly, when I implemented a similar practice with my young daughter, she reacted much the same way! So, when she'd ask, I'd stop and pay full attention to her, even if it was for a short period of time. After experimenting for a few days, the evidence was clear. She needed L.O.V.E.

Learning to listen with L.O.V.E. is a simple, yet powerful, method to enhance communication and deepen our connection with our kids. When we listen with L.O.V.E., it conveys our desire and willingness to connect with our children. And, giving them our undivided attention is the best way to validate them as individuals. Listening with L.O.V.E. involves the following steps and can be adopted to children of various ages: **Listen, Observe, Validate, and Engage.**

LISTEN: The first and most important step is to stop: stop what you're doing and just listen. It may seem simple, but it's a challenge in our multi-tasking, busier-than-ever culture. In order to listen, stop whatever you're doing, turn toward your child, and look at her. She wants to see your eyes looking her way. You want her to know she has your full attention. Even better is when you also take a step or two closer to her and lean in. Now your goal is just to listen to whatever she's saying . . . without interrupting . . . just listening.

OBSERVE: While you're in this posture, pay attention to her non-verbal as well as verbal communication. What mood is she in? What expression is on her face? How quickly is she talking compared to how she normally talks? Your response will largely be determined by what you're observing.

VALIDATE: When she has finished talking, acknowledge her comments and validate what she said. Either restate it or ask a clarifying question. Provide affirmation by letting her know you heard and understood what she said. Avoid jumping into the conversation without first taking this step. It's possible you'll find out what you heard wasn't really what she intended to communicate. When you're on the same page, effort isn't wasted on miscommunication, and you're both less likely to become frustrated.

ENGAGE: After you've listened, observed, and validated, then look to engage in conversation and convey your understanding, wisdom, or sage advice, if necessary. Now you've earned that right and whatever you say is more likely to be received as intended.

Far too often we are quick to engage without first truly listening with a desire to understand. One of Stephen R. Covey's seven principles in his book, *7 Habits of Highly Effective People,* is to seek first to understand, then to be understood. The principle applies equally to children and adults.

Ironically, depending on the child and the topic of discussion, after practicing this method, there may be times when you don't even have to engage. Your child will appreciate your attention to such a degree you won't need to say anything. She'll have felt listened to . . . and it felt good! That was all she needed.

REFLECTION AND DISCUSSION QUESTIONS:

1. Notice your body language now when your children talk to you. Do they have your full attention? How would you describe your current listening habits?
2. What's getting in the way of you becoming a better listener?

ACTION STEPS:

1. Rehearse with the L.O.V.E. steps in your mind and see yourself listening in that manner.
2. Make it a practice this week to listen with L.O.V.E. each time your children speak to you.

GET PERMISSION TO TALK

Do you ever want your children's attention when they are in the middle of doing something else? Depending upon what they're involved with, getting them to stop and listen can be challenging. But sometimes you *need* to get their attention, which will mean interrupting them. Too often, this interaction and disruption of whatever they are involved with leads to conflict.

Chances are, if you start observing what's working and what's not, you'll agree that in these situations, a different approach may be in order. If you follow this example, like me, you may find a few changes make a big difference.

First, before speaking to my son, for example, I need to observe what he is doing. Is he watching television, doing homework, playing a video game, or texting? Whatever he's involved with shouldn't affect my reaction. It shouldn't matter how much or little I value the activity. For instance, if I think what he's watching on TV is a waste of time, it'll be reflected in my tone. However, at this moment, his choice of television show has nothing to do with what I currently want (i.e., his attention), so it's likely something to discuss another time, if that's a concern.

Then, ask permission . . . yes, ask permission. At first, you may think this is self-demeaning. Why should we have to ask permission, right? Wrong! Kids are people, too. What they are doing, even if it's nothing, may not be significant to us, but it's important to them . . . and that's what we want to recognize. So, if we're interested in having a meaningful exchange and avoiding unnecessary conflict, this step is worth the two seconds it takes.

I can ask permission by just saying, for example, "Hey, son." I'll be able to get his attention, without rudely interrupting what he's doing. Remember, whether I value what he's doing at the moment is irrelevant! After I say his name, I'll wait for a response. Wait means to stand (not hover) or sit close by and wait. I can't walk away or start doing anything else until after I've had an exchange. So, I'll just wait. He needs to know I'm not going to go away, or get distracted, until he's responded to me.

If after five seconds he ignores my request, I'll ask one more time by simply making a statement such as, "Son, can I have your attention?" Then I'll stand and wait . . . without moving. At this point, I'll want to make sure I'm at least in his peripheral vision. The reaction I'm looking for is for him to stop or pause whatever he's doing and acknowledge me in return.

Once he's tuned in, I'll start talking and say, "I have something to ask you," or, "I have something to ask you; can you pay attention for a minute?" I'm seeking buy-in and his approval to communicate. I know, you may be thinking, *You're just talking to a child; it really shouldn't take this much effort.* Well, are we are serious about enhancing our communication and connection with our children? If the answer is yes, then we'll want to afford them this respect that we would appreciate if we were in their shoes. (And remember, our goal is to teach effective communication skills, as well.)

If my son is very engrossed in what he's doing, then I might initiate a light touch to get his attention, which should suffice. I want him to be looking at me, so I can look him in the eyes when I'm talking, or at least know he's listening. (There is some research to indicate some boys don't respond well if eye contact is required, so take that into consideration.) But, if I start talking without him being aware, then we'll both end up frustrated, and the exchange will be less effective and less productive. What could have been an opportunity for connection now ends in conflict.

If at all possible, avoid hollering across the house or up the stairs. I'll actually make the effort to walk upstairs, instead of just yelling. Not only is it more impactful, but it also subtly communicates that I care enough to take the extra time and energy (and I get a few more steps in for the day, as well). However, if it's necessary for some reason, then we want to pay close attention to our tone of voice. But whenever possible, I'll try to be in the same room and reasonably close, without hovering. Once I've been acknowledged and have agreement to listen, the stage has been set and I'm able to proceed with my question and into our engagement and discussion.

Remember, I'm trying to model the behavior I want him to emulate. How would I want him to approach me when I'm in the middle of working, exercising, getting ready for work, relaxing, reading, or whatever?

Since you're the parent, you may feel like this method is undignified or that it shouldn't be necessary because you have the authority. However, if we're genuinely desiring to have meaningful and productive exchanges with our children, then this approach is worth the effort. Maybe you think this process seems a bit technical or rehearsed or time consuming. Well, that's because it is. The goal is intentional effort to achieve a better result.

Of course, you're not breaking a cardinal rule if you don't apply this approach in every situation, but try it on occasion and see what you think. By following these steps, the process will go much more quickly than you anticipate. You'll have more meaningful exchanges, and your connection will remain intact and will even be strengthened.

Reflection and Discussion Questions:

1. How did it make you feel when you read this section about how to engage with your children and secure their attention when needed?

2. What changes do you notice in your dialogue when you implement these steps?

ACTION STEPS:

1. Become aware of how you currently initiate conversations with your children when they're doing some activity.
2. Practice these steps: Observe, Ask Permission, Wait for a Response, Engage.

Mean What You Say

Y ou've just made a comment without first thinking it through. Words flew out of your mouth you now wish you could recapture. If you're like most people, it happened when you were frustrated or annoyed or angry. Perhaps you were running late. Maybe you had other things you'd rather have been doing. Or perhaps your kid was doing something that just bugged you.

Scenarios like these usually result in a bad outcome. We can make comments we don't really mean to say, and we can come across speaking meanly, even if that's not our intent.

Remember, between stimulus and response is our unique human ability to choose our response. You'd probably agree, taking a split second to think about what you're going to say saves a lot of wasted energy and produces a better outcome. No matter what trips our trigger, we can still reflect first, instead of automatically reacting and saying something we regret.

Also, when we think before speaking, we're more likely to mean what we say. As a result, it's important to then follow through on what we've said. In an effort to be effective communicators, we're establishing a pattern that our words carry significance and will lead to either a positive or negative consequence.

For example, if I tell my son I'm going to leave in five minutes, I need to be ready to leave in five minutes, whether he is or not. But I have to make sure I can really leave him alone if he's not ready to leave when I say I'm leaving. If that's not the case, then it wasn't a wise choice of words. As you can see, not only are there consequences for him, but for me, as well.

What we say is important. We're establishing and reinforcing trust with our children. We want them to know they can trust us because they've learned we mean what we say.

For example, if my child is persisting in asking for help with something or wanting to play, and I say, "I'll be there in five minutes," then I will do my best to be there in five minutes. Again, we're building trust and modeling the behavior we want our children to replicate. So, the main thing to recognize is that if we don't mean it, we simply mustn't say it.

In the same way, we want to be on guard and take every precaution to avoid making threats—even idle ones we don't intend to carry out. People with a controlling nature are especially prone to this habit. But our children quickly learn that we really don't mean it if we say something like, "If you don't clean up your room, I'll never, ever buy you a piece of clothing again!"

Occasionally, we can't do what we've said we're going to do. In those situations, we again 'fess up, admit it, and apologize. Our children will appreciate our contrition . . . even if they don't like it.

No matter what, even when we say what we mean, there really isn't any occasion when it's necessary to say it meanly. Is that how you want to be spoken to? I'm sure not! It's good to be reminded of the instruction provided in Colossians 3:21, which says, "Fathers, don't aggravate your children. If you do, they will become discouraged and quit trying."

The better alternative is to always say what we mean, but to never say it meanly. James, the brother of Jesus, provided wise and practical advice in James 1:19 when he reminded us, "My dear brothers and sisters, be quick to listen, slow to speak, and slow to get angry." Our children will quickly learn to appreciate and respect that approach, and the results are always better.

Reflection and Discussion Questions:

1. Has there been a time recently that you now regret when you spoke without thinking first? What was the result of that interaction?

2. Are you currently consistent and intentional in meaning what you say each time you talk or ask something of your children? What's a change you can make?

Action Steps:

1. If needed, practice stopping and thinking for a brief moment before you speak.

2. Be conscious of asking yourself if what you're about to say is going to produce the result you want and if you're able to mean what you say.

PRINCIPLE 12
CHOOSE NOT TO LECTURE

No one likes to be lectured, including me. How about you?

If we don't like to be spoken to in that manner, then it makes sense that lecturing probably isn't an effective parenting strategy. We don't want lecturing, and the need to continually repeat what we've said, to be part of our parenting repertoire. . . and is never desirable. If we find the need to continually repeat or belabor the points we've said, then something has gone wrong in the communication chain.

Repeating generally refers to when we make requests or ask our children to do something more than once, whereas belaboring or lecturing usually happens when the parent insists on trying to make a point. Either way, anyone on the receiving end of either hearing something repeated or being lectured becomes a tune-out specialist. Have you noticed it doesn't take long for children to learn to ignore the parent who repeats and lectures? Kids are quick to recognize that responding really won't stop the barrage of words coming at them.

The unfortunate result of continually repeating ourselves is that we can quickly feel disrespected and become frustrated due to the effort exerted. In turn, the child—no matter what age—who is having to listen to the repetition also doesn't feel respected and becomes frustrated. And the scenario can even escalate as parents will often begin to demean or insult a child without even being aware of it.

If you have experience nagging or lecturing your children, have you found it to be an effective method of affecting change? Think about it, when someone only points out what you're doing wrong, are you inspired to want to change? Probably not, right? Most likely, all the talking does is make you defensive. Our children are no different; in fact, they are probably affected more since their emotional capacity hasn't fully developed.

If we're continually repeating what we say, thinking it will motivate our children, it's helpful to <u>first</u> identify what *we* might be able to do differently, not how our *children* need to change. By becoming more aware of how we're communicating, we're then able to present our requests differently. The beauty is that when we're able to create a better initial connection, we're less likely to feel we have to belabor the point and can refrain from piling on. Not sure if you have a habit of repeating, belaboring, or lecturing? Ask your children. They might gladly give you a hint. Be aware, however, that only when we've established a high level of trust, without fear of reprisal, will our children feel safe enough to give us an honest response. If trust is lacking, then any feedback we ask for will most likely not generate an authentic response. Our kids want us to see them in the best light, so they'll tell us what we want to hear, unless they know they can be forthright, and not pay a price for being honest.

REFLECTION AND DISCUSSION QUESTIONS:

1. How would you currently describe in general your words and your tone, and is it different for each child? Do you come across to your kids as if you're lecturing?

2. If so, what can you change to come across in a healthier manner?

ACTION STEPS:

1. Assess how often your children listen and respond to your request the first time you ask them and track how often you become frustrated by having to repeat yourself.
2. Intentionally and consistently change how you talk, as needed, and identify the improvements you experience.

PRINCIPLE 13
KEEP MISTAKES IN PERSPECTIVE

Helping our children develop healthy habits when they are young will set them up for success as they grow and mature. It's been said: "We make our habits, and then our habits make us." The point is that even our children's "little" habits, like not picking up after themselves or procrastinating on homework, can become part of their identity and infiltrate into other unwanted behaviors, which can carry much more significance.

But after telling our kids 100 times to hang up their belongings and we still find the floor littered with coats and shoes, we're bound to be exasperated and wonder why they don't listen to us and do as we ask. In situations like these, it's common to feel disappointed in our children. Unfortunately, if we feel that way, we can fall into the habit of admonishing our children in a very condemning tone. And that's not a healthy habit, either!

When we identify habits that won't serve our children well as an adult, it's our responsibility as parents to step in and redirect the path they are on. How we respond during these times determines how our children will react and, in fact, learn and grow. Although seemingly easier, ignoring negative behaviors (which will likely result in character flaws), is never the answer. But neither is coming across in a judgmental or condemning manner. We can be right about something, but if we're shaming in how we admonish our kids, it's always the wrong method to use. As loving parents, we have a much higher standard and calling.

It's important to remember, much like for us, "mistakes" kids make are often just habits that develop—not character defects. However, when we come across as condemning or shaming, it crosses the line by making them feel attacked and injuring their spirit, which only makes matters worse. Depending on the personality of your children, they may react and let you know how they feel. Or they may not respond outwardly at all. Inwardly, however, they'll begin to question their own self-worth. Remember, if we continually criticize or shame our children, they don't stop loving us. They stop loving *themselves*.

In her book, *Shame Lifter*, author Marilyn Hontz shares her experiences of being shamed as a child. She states, "You can identify shame givers by the way they listen to you and the words they use. First, look at the way a shame giver listens to you. They are not good listeners. They may hear your words, but they do not hear your heart. They are listening to you only so they may try to 'fix' the problem instead of *listening to understand* where you are coming from. There is a big difference between 'listening to fix' and "listening to understand." She goes on to identify these other traits of shame givers:

- Shame givers are more interested in your performance than in who you are.
- Shame givers interrupt.
- Shame givers' words tend to be discouraging and frequently use the word *should*.
- Shame givers communicate an "I know better than you" attitude.

- Shame givers use words that have a way of labeling you.
- Shame givers are quick to give out put-downs.
- Shame givers can sound like scolding parents.
- Shame givers make true statements in jest.
- Shame givers make negative comments without considering their words before they make them.

Many situations that occur, from the time our kids are little through their teenage years, don't require words of admonishment or correction, especially if the misstep was accidental and not intentional. If my young child spills his milk on the floor, does he really need me yelling at him for the accident? Although it's not guaranteed, kids usually know when they've messed up and feel bad enough about what happened without any further judgment coming from us. Harsh words or a disciplinary response won't do anything to make the situation better.

Making ourselves feel better, more superior, or in control by being the judge and jury is the wrong approach and not something we want as a parenting trademark. We can learn to keep our perspective and learn to correct and encourage and enforce without judging or condemning or shaming. Using an approach focused on building-up and encouraging is much more productive and produces long-term changes most beneficial for our children.

Always remember this phrase. . . "It's not about me!" It's about what's in the best interest of our children.

Reflection and Discussion Questions:

1. What is behind your words—how are you feeling when you're communicating? What's the emotion beneath the surface?
2. How can you change to avoid coming across in a condemning or belittling manner when you find your children doing something wrong?

ACTION STEPS:

1. Listen to the words you say and discern your intended meaning when correcting or just talking to your kids after they make a mistake.

2. Identify what steps can you implement to prevent them from making mistakes.

ESTABLISH EXPECTATIONS AND CONSEQUENCES

Just as a loving God disciplines his children, we know that discipline is essential for the well-being of our children. However, as parents, we can often become frustrated and feel unsuccessful at enforcing discipline. If you're like Christy and me, you've probably discussed and tried many different approaches to correct your children. Regardless, there are occasions when it seemed like nothing we tried worked, no matter what methods we attempted.

What we found was that many of the areas of conflict arising in our home revolved around the same few issues. So, we came to a logical conclusion that there is probably a more effective way to discipline, especially since we could almost predict which areas were going to lead to disagreement, frustration, and conflict.

In stepping back, we realized we hadn't taken time to set up a framework we could rely and depend on to help with this problem. An effective yet often overlooked strategy we implemented was to design the consequences ahead of time. It involved a two-step process. First, we outlined the expectations in advance. Second, we identified their consequences.

If you're not already using this method, start paying attention to the situations causing the conflict in your home, especially those that are being repeated. For us, it usually involved disputes about doing homework, cleaning up their rooms, putting coats and shoes away, and doing dishes. Sometimes issues may include bigger concerns like coming home late, driving too fast, talking back, poor effort, or being selfish.

With the goal of achieving a shared understanding between you and your children, discuss the common issues with them. You're now positioned to establish expectations and consequences with them beforehand. Once initiated, be committed to the process and, above all, be consistent. This strategy won't work effectively if there is any level of inconsistency.

If you're committed to giving this a try, be aware that it'll be too big a leap if you initiate too many changes at the same time. Instead, pick one or two problem areas you can consistently manage and start there. Once you feel you have done well with those areas, you can add in others.

As an example, some of our kids had developed the habit of leaving shoes lying around the house. To help solve the issue, I installed four shelves in the garage just outside the mudroom. Each of our four children had their own shelf on which to put their shoes. We showed each of them their shelf. Now they knew where to put their shoes before coming inside.

We then laid out the consequence: they owed us twenty-five cents any time we found their shoes lying around the house. From that point forward, if we found shoes in the house, we picked them up, showed them the shoes, and collected the quarter on the spot. Of course, to reinforce the behavior, they still had to take their shoes and put them on the shelf. It only took a couple times of collecting coins before abandoned shoes became a non-issue. When we did find an occasional pair of shoes in the house unattended, it was back to them picking up and putting away their shoes and us collecting spare change.

Taking a little time to think through a solution, and establishing and communicating the expectations and consequences ahead of time, saves lots of frustration and conflict on the back end. Yes, it will take effort initially, and don't expect perfection. Be flexible and willing to modify as you learn more about what works and what doesn't. Over time, you'll be glad you did.

REFLECTION AND DISCUSSION QUESTIONS:

1. How consistent have you been up to this point in your parenting with establishing and enforcing consequences?

2. Were your own parents consistent in giving you consequences as a kid? Think about your parents' parenting style. How does their methodology influence how you parent?

ACTION STEPS:

1. Identify what areas are continual sources of conflict. Brainstorm and come up with logical and easy to administer consequences.

2. Meet with your children and review the points of notable conflict and the suggested consequences and reach an understanding, if not agreement. Then be consistent.

ASSESS YOUR WORD RATIO

Have you ever tracked how many times you correct, criticize, or condemn versus the number of times you compliment your children? Face it. Children are always going to be doing something wrong. In fact, I don't know any of us who are perfect.

But how often do we expect perfection from our children and point out to them when they're not perfect? Or, how many times do we point out things they do wrong or could have done better? Alternatively, how frequently do we observe and acknowledge when they do something right and make good choices?

The research by Dr. John Gottman on married couples is significant and can be applied to our relationship with our children (or anyone else), as well. In studying married couples, the researchers were able to predict which couples would stay together and those who would split by looking at the ratio of compliments to criticism. It was determined that the healthiest relationships exhibited a compliment to criticism ratio of 5:1. So, for every one criticism the partner conveyed, five compliments were needed to offset their criticism.

If we apply this premise to our parenting, we can assess our compliment to criticism ratio toward our children. In order to see how we're doing, a simple strategy is to keep track of our ratio for three days in a row. Be prepared: if my results were any indication, you may be embarrassed. We often have no idea how we're doing until we monitor it. Initially, I thought I was delivering mainly positive comments, only to discover the opposite.

If you do this and find your ratio is less than 5:1, don't be discouraged . . . you're in good company, unfortunately. Sad to say, it's not our nature to be intentional about complimenting family members. We're much more likely to encourage our kids' friends than our own children . . . it's just how some of us are wired. But becoming an encourager (like many traits) is a skill that, with intentional focus, can change rather quickly.

As a practical example, there was a period when Christy and I became concerned about how critical our daughter was being toward her siblings. I admonished her for it a couple of times. But then, I felt prompted to examine if there was something I was doing to contribute to her attitude. Very quickly, I recognized I'd become complacent in my words of encouragement and recognition toward her, which is what feeds her soul and is part of her love language.

Over the next couple days, I was very intentional about spreading words of worthy praise, affection, and encouragement to her. The carryover was dramatic. She was passing out what she'd been getting. Suddenly, she became less critical and much more patient toward her siblings.

What kind of atmosphere do you want to establish in your home? Which do you think is more appealing for the parent and child—a home filled with more compliments, or one with criticism? The comments are yours to convey, and the environment is yours to create.

REFLECTION AND DISCUSSION QUESTIONS:

1. What is your compliment to criticism ratio with your spouse? With your children?

2. What is your motivation in pointing out to your kids that they're doing things wrong? Can you see how criticism isn't the correct approach, especially if they're not receiving adequate and appropriate encouragement?

ACTION STEPS:

1. For three days, track your compliment to criticism/correction ratio.

2. Look for and reinforce when you see your kids doing something right and when you find the need to correct, or slip and say something in a negative tone, be intentional about also saying at least two or more positive words of encouragement or find a way to compliment.

TaKe TiMe To EnJoy

Most parents can recall watching and listening to the peaceful, rhythmic breathing of their infant child lying quietly in the crib. Except for their crinkled face, accompanying the occasional gas emission, that little bundle was adoringly peaceful.

In those moments, it's easy to be joyful and thankful for the blessing of the new life lying in front of us We wouldn't even think of judging, cajoling, correcting, or condemning; we just bask in awesome wonder.

But as our children get older, how often do we sit back, watch, and admire our children? Seldom do parents take time to just relax, observe, enjoy, and be filled with wonderment. Unfortunately, it seems as if we can forget how much joy children can give us.

Parenting is hard! I don't know anything more challenging. Nothing I've experienced in the work world is more demanding than parenting. Part of the reason is because we care so much. You see, it's only the people or things we care about that stimulate strong emotions.

And because we care so much, we can easily find the need to be continually correcting and telling our kids what they could be doing better.

But what's worse, often we aren't even mentally present enough to notice what they are doing.

As an unflattering example, I recall my young daughter saying, "Hey, Daddy, come sit down and watch me dance." Often, I'd reluctantly sit on the sofa while she cranked up the music, entering her fantasy world. It was pure joy for her. She was doing what she loved, for the person she loved, while desiring my love in return.

But was I really giving her what she wanted or needed? Was I sitting and watching . . . and taking in the joy she was offering me? Or, was my mind preoccupied and not even in the room? Regrettably, I recall missing too many moments, which will never be recaptured.

Do your kids play piano or a musical instrument? Are they involved in sports? Do they participate in drama? Do they play video games? If you want to do yourself and your children a favor, and create a mutually meaningful experience, find the occasions when you do what you did when your children were infants . . . just enjoy.

When your child is playing the piano, for example, what if you sat close by and simply enjoyed the music, without correcting . . . or cringing? Just take pleasure in the playing. Watch the fingers glance quickly from key to key and marvel at the focus and concentration, regardless of the sounds emanating from the instrument.

When you attend your child's athletic event, allow yourself to sit in the stands and enjoy every movement without mentally criticizing or retaining what he or she did wrong so you can advise on what to do better. Permit your mind to be filled with joy and pride solely because he or she is out there participating in the sport.

After each of these activities, we can sincerely tell our children we loved or had fun watching them play and how proud we are they're participating. In the same instant, we have to resist the urge to add comments about what they could have done better (there will be a different time and place to be the coach, if it's necessary at all). For now, we can just take time to enjoy the beautiful gift of life God has brought into our lives.

REFLECTION AND DISCUSSION QUESTIONS:

1. How did you feel when you read about this strategy? How different or similar is it to how you currently observe your kids' participation in activities?
2. Are you able to just sit and observe and enjoy watching your kids perform, or do you become anxious, judgmental, or worried about how they'll perform?

ACTION STEPS:

1. Find an opportunity to catch your kids doing something they love to do—an activity they participate in or practice. Sit without any distraction (put your phone away) and take in the event with the intent to just enjoy it.
2. After their next practice or performance, resist the urge to correct, criticize, or coach. Only comment on how much you enjoyed watching them participate and how proud you are of them.

LET LIFE TEACH THE LESSON

I f you're like me, you want your kids to succeed and avoid making mistakes you made. As a result, it's instinctive to quickly jump in and help or protect them so they won't fail or be embarrassed.

The level at which we do this may vary. For instance, sometimes thinking I was helping, I'd finish my son's homework, so he wouldn't be late with it or fail the assignment. And, at one point, I'd repeatedly go in to wake him up, so he wasn't late for school.

To take this example further, when one of our sons started high school, he had to be ready for school by 7:00 a.m. His freshman year, he set his watch alarm and was up early and ready to go. At some point during his sophomore year, I found myself going to his room at 6:15 a.m. and again at 6:25 a.m. and again at 6:35 a.m. to awaken him. I was frustrated because it interrupted my morning. And I became irritated at him for not being more responsible.

Something had to change. So, we had a talk. He needed to understand his decision to not get up on time impacted my morning routine. And, it affected him because he'd end up rushing, eating breakfast too quickly, and hurrying out the door. At the time, he was catching a ride with his best friend. So, he'd often be late getting to his house, which caused his friend anxiety as well. I explained that every time he showed up late, he was being unreliable and irresponsible. Was that really what he wanted his best friend to think of him?

It was important for him to see his decisions affected other people, as is almost always the case. In addition, his decisions also damaged his reputation. There's a reason Proverbs 22:1 says, "Choose a good reputation over great riches. Being held in high esteem is better than silver and gold."

To resolve the situation, I told him for the following week, if needed, I'd come up one time and no more. If he didn't get up and was late and missed his ride, it was on him to figure out how to get to school. That was all it took, in this case. He responded wonderfully; he felt better and so did I.

As you can see, it's apparent that if we care more about the outcome (e.g., getting to school on time) than our children do, no one benefits. To do so means we're taking on responsibility that is not ours, and robbing our kids of the opportunity to develop, grow, and mature.

My youngest daughter overall does a very good job of getting herself out of bed and ready for school. One morning, when she was running just a bit behind schedule, it was my turn to give her a ride to school on my way to work. I had the car warmed up and was sitting in it ready to go. After a few minutes she came dashing out the door. We'd driven for a few minutes when she realized she'd left her student ID at home. (They won't let her in the school without her ID.) I didn't say much other than, "Well, I guess we have to go back and get it." So we did a U-turn and headed back home to pick it up. Of course, by now the threat of both of us being late was becoming a reality. This time, with ID in hand, we headed back to school. If this happened to you, how would you respond?

I could tell she was upset with herself for leaving her ID behind and now possibly making me late for work. From my recollection, she'd forgotten things before, but it was a rare occurrence. We'd driven for about five minutes and she said, "I'm sorry Dad. I hope you're not late." She was more concerned about me having to drive further and being late than she was about herself. From her reaction and her words, it was evident that she knew she forgot it because she was rushing and not prepared ... and it bothered her and she owned it. No admonition from me was necessary. Her not being ready to go on time caused the problem and being late for school was the consequence she was about to pay.

Certainly, there are times we are compelled to step in and protect and offer a safety net. But often, we need to step back and allow life to be the teacher. It's the best way our children learn basic truths–like all decisions have consequences. It's a powerful reality that, if learned early, will benefit them immeasurably for the rest of their life.

REFLECTION AND DISCUSSION QUESTIONS:

1. When and how often do find yourself repeating and reminding your kids because you don't want to be embarrassed or inconvenienced?
2. Do you tend to step in and finish a task your kids have started? If so, why?

ACTION STEPS:

1. Identify some situations when you've been jumping in to "help" but will now let life be the teacher.
2. Let your children know the changes that you'll be making and why it's important for them to learn from their mistakes and choices.

CONNECT BEFORE YOU CORRECT

Y ou'll hear it often. I'm guilty of it, sometimes. It's a bad habit and tears down relationships. It's felt immediately, but often goes unrecognized. What am I talking about?

It happens in the home and in work settings, between loved ones and between friends, and it's always destructive. What is it? I'm talking about the tendency to correct BEFORE connecting. There are countless times when it is necessary to correct our children. But often, kids on the receiving end will feel like corrections and criticism are all they hear.

- It happens when our kids come home from school and we tell them to hang up their backpacks and coats BEFORE we welcome them home and greet them with a hug.
- It happens when we point out the messy kitchen that begs to be cleaned BEFORE we express appreciation for the effort they made to prepare the food.
- It happens on the phone when we call our kids to check in on how they're doing, but instead we immediately launch into an

interrogation to see if they've done their chores and homework BEFORE we connect with a proper greeting.

To counter and minimize our reactions when these occasions occur, we'd be wise to become intentional about the words we say before we spout corrections. Rather than immediately sermonizing about what our kids did wrong and start correcting, we'll make better headway by first initiating the exchange with some basic small talk or with a hug.

Properly acknowledging our children before we point out what they didn't do yet or did wrong is a much better strategy. Anytime we put results BEFORE relationships, we've demonstrated our inability to lead and influence effectively.

Relationships matter. If we want to grow our relationship with our children, we'll be well served to become aware and make this one simple, but profound, shift . . . CONNECT before we CORRECT. Correcting the problem before connecting to them first means we see them as a problem to be fixed, instead of a child to be cherished.

Just think about it . . . how do you feel when a boss or supervisor starts out your meetings or reviews with what you've done wrong, without acknowledging something positive that you've accomplished? Are you more inclined to immediately want to do better, or allow some level of resentment to creep in. If it happens once, you'll probably let it slide, but if it's a reoccurring pattern of his or her leadership style, you'll probably wish you had a different supervisor, or will go start looking for one.

If you're a reader of the New Testament, you've probably noticed how the Apostle Paul often starts his letters with words of appreciation and encouragement. Even though he had to communicate via written letters, he was thoughtful and built them up by making a positive connection, before he would request something or point out and correct mistakes they were making, as new Christ followers.

And when you follow Paul's example and connect before you correct, here's the unexpected benefit: You'll find the results you were looking for will come with much less conflict and resistance and you'll gain cooperation in return. It's a beautiful thing when we can grow our relationships AND get the desired results!

REFLECTION AND DISCUSSION QUESTIONS:

1. Are there times when you habitually start giving orders or making requests before you establish a connection? When do these times most frequently occur?
2. How would you describe your current relationship with your children and what changes would you like to see?

ACTION STEPS:

1. Tomorrow, when your children get up in the morning or come home from school, pay attention to how you initially greet them.
2. After making this change, identify the differences you're noticing in your relationship with your children.

PRINCIPLE 19
SEEK TO CREATE MEMORIES

To really speak into the hearts of our children, often it's not what we say that leaves an impression, but what we in fact do—especially when it's unexpected. Who doesn't like surprises, right!? As you'll continually hear me say, words matter . . . a lot. But so do our actions. If you're verbose, this is especially true

One simple way to make an indelible mark is by asking our children what they'd like to do and then do it. We can do this one-on-one or with multiple children, if they agree on the activity. Perhaps you're already in the habit of doing this. If so, good for you, and keep it up! When we ask them, what we want is for them to pick an activity of their choice. Hopefully they'll chose one of their favorite activities and allow us to actively participate in their enjoyment. You may need to set parameters at the outset by saying something like, "I have 15 minutes, what would you like to do?" Depending on the age of your child, even five minutes of uninterrupted play time with you can create quite an impression.

An adaptation of this strategy is when we find our children already engaged in an activity. Then we can simply ask permission to join them. I've also found the impression I make is even more significant when I participate in activities I don't normally do, or engage in games or sports that are way outside my comfort zone. (I'm not suggesting you do anything that will get you injured or maimed, so use your judgment.)

What kids remember are experiences, especially those that create an emotional connection. One-on-one experiences are best, when it's possible, but don't make that the rule. Shared work can build wonderful bonds and memories. One summer, we decided to get rid of the juniper bushes that had gotten out of control and were too close to our house. After we had trimmed off and bagged all the branches, the boys and I started digging out the stumps and as many of the roots as we could. After having labored for hours in the hot sun, there was a shared feeling of accomplishment, pride, and joy that exploded in high-fives as we made the final chop to remove the last stump . . . it was priceless.

In addition to creating these scenarios throughout the normal course of a day, we can also look for unique opportunities to engage in experiences outside of our regular daily life. For example, after they graduated high school, I took each of our boys on a wilderness retreat called "Adventures in Fatherhood." It was a group of about 20 dads who each brought a son or daughter. The group was broken into five pairs who, along with two trained guides, spent four days in a remote wilderness location. We camped, slept under the stars in our sleeping bags, rock climbed, repelled, and did cliff diving. There was also the opportunity to go off alone in the woods with your child and spend four hours just talking! Many who attended couldn't remember the last time they had spent four hours alone with their child, let alone just to talk.

Chances are your kids have activities they like to do or sports in which they are already participating. Or, perhaps you'll have an opportunity to help them become involved and learn a new sport or activity. Golf is a sport that I enjoy, but didn't play much after we started having kids. When our youngest daughter was in junior high, I introduced her to golf and gradually she took a liking to it. Since then, we've been able to enjoy wonderful experiences both practicing and playing golf. I'm confident she'll always fondly recall our playing times together.

We're well served to remember that our children remember and relish experiences more than what we say. When our children look back at their childhood, it won't be all the things we told them they'll recall first. It'll be things we did with them that created memories and were appreciated, especially those that were unexpected.

Reflection and Discussion Questions:

1. What are activities your children like to do that you could do with them?
2. Are there activities your children like to do that you've never done with them and would surprise them if you ask to do it with them?

Action Steps:

1. Set a goal to engage with your kids in their chosen activity at least once per week.
2. When you've concluded the activity, be sure to state how much you enjoyed the time and activity with them and look forward to doing it again.

FOCUS ON THE PROCESS

O ur personality, which is partially shaped by our past experiences, will influence our mindset and the way we communicate with our children. When you were growing up, what did your parents emphasize when it came to performance? Were they outcome-driven or process-driven? Both process and outcomes are important. But since we can only control the process, and not the result, our energy is better spent by focusing on the process.

Without going into the psychology behind how people are shaped, it's pivotal to recognize this very important concept. When communicating with our children, it's worthwhile to focus on the preparation and process, not on the outcome. In other words, in almost every circumstance, our children can control their effort much more than what happens.

With this as the premise, we want to be careful about what we say in response to what our children do. The words we say, and what we emphasize, will shape what our children value and on what they concentrate. Believe it or not, they can sense what's important to us, even if it may not seem like it at times! So, if they feel we value outcomes versus preparation and effort, then they will derive their sense of worth by the results they produce. That is a dangerous precedent to set.

When I talk about outcome, I'm referring to the *result* of the action or activity. This is different than the process, which is *how* something gets done. A further distinction is to say that process emphasizes the effort, determination, and dedication that go into producing a good result. When we center on the outcome, and ignore the process, we're sending the message that we're not that concerned with how the job gets done, only that the outcome is sufficient in our eyes. We have to be really careful here, because we could unintentionally convey that it's okay to get the proper result no matter the cost, or how it's done.

A simple illustration was when our teenage daughter would fix her hair. Some mornings before school, she'd take extra time and either curl or in some way style her hair. I could say, "Your hair looks great today." But, a better choice is to say, "I like what you did with your hair today." In the second statement, it's easy to see how the emphasis is on the effort, not the outcome. The first statement conveyed I valued how she looks, whereas the second statement places value on the effort she took to fix her hair.

As another example, let's look at grades. The words we say can convey we're more interested in having our kids get As on their report card than in establishing good study habits. Good study habits are the process and As are the outcome. This one is difficult for many parents, especially those who want to see their kids excel academically.

We're trained to view success by how good of grades our kids get. But what message are we sending with our words? Are we focused on what is in their best interest long term? Good study habits will serve them well as they progress through their educational process. I know this from experience. I got mostly all As in high school—was on the honor roll and all that. Unfortunately, I almost flunked out my first semester in college, because I'd not learned <u>how</u> to study!

This is such an important point that I feel more examples are necessary to illustrate this concept:

- Are you more interested in your kids just getting their homework done, or that what is penned looks neat enough for the teacher to read? Writing neatly is the process, while having the assignment completed is the outcome. Both are important but developing the right process (penmanship, in this example) will insure a more consistent outcome no matter what the task.

- Would you rather have your children play in the game, or possess a positive attitude regardless of how many minutes they play? Possessing a positive attitude is the process whereas playing in the game is the outcome.

- Are you more interested in having your kids get to school before the bell rings, or in them getting up on time and allowing margin to get ready, eat breakfast, and arrive early? Being up on time and allowing margin is the process whereas being to school before the bell rings is the outcome.

What matters is for our children to learn they can always control the amount of effort they put into something, but they can't always control the outcome. To put the focus on what they can't control can be very discouraging.

In math, for example, a child may be very gifted, so he doesn't need to try very hard to excel in high school. But what if he ends up in college with a lot of other very smart kids, with some being more gifted than he is in math? Now, instead of being at the top of his class and getting As, he's in the middle of the class and getting Cs.

These situations can also often lead to comparisons, which is almost always a problem. In almost every context, there will be somebody who is stronger, faster, smarter, better looking, funnier, more spiritual, taller, thinner, or more compassionate and caring. Many kids will respond by thinking they're a failure and lose motivation. Unfortunately, they haven't learned that process and effort are what improves performance. The irony is that when we take pressure off our kids by not focusing on the outcomes or results, they actually perform better.

A well-known saying states, "How we do anything is how we do everything." By emphasizing the process—how things get done—we're preparing our kids in a manner that will serve them well through the different stages of life, and they'll have more consistent, positive outcomes, in everything they do. We're well served to remember that our children aren't machines to perform for us, but rather souls to be nurtured and loved.

ReFLeCTION anD DISCUSSION QUeSTIONS:

1. Do you have a tendency to compare your children to others? Do they feel that it's difficult to live up to the standards you have for them?

2. Are there past situations, related to this principle, for which apologizing to your kids would be in order?

ACTION STePS:

1. Analyze the words you use and assess whether emphasis is placed on outcome or effort and, in advance, pick word choices to use and rephrase what you say, so you acknowledge their choices, effort, and decisions, not the outcome you want them to have.

2. Engage your children in a discussion allowing them to express when they feel pressured to perform or achieve a specific outcome.

MONITOR YOUR SELF-TALK

From the moment we were born, every message we received was recorded in our brain. Depending on your upbringing, and your home environment, that might be a comforting thought or a scary one. The same is true for our children. So, what's being stamped into their brain?

Regardless of how we grew up, researchers have estimated up to 77 percent of the mental programs we have are false, harmful, or work against us. Guess what! Unfortunately, we pass many of them on to our children!

Like learning to speak, our mental programs were adopted from listening to those around us, without discerning if the messages were positive or negative, true or false, or in our best interest. Our well-meaning parents probably gave us some of the messages. Others came to us through coaches or teachers or friends who didn't understand the impact that words have on young minds. Many of the messages we received weren't true and were, in fact, damaging.

In the brain, each time a message is received, a pathway is created—a physical, chemical, "neural pathway" that gets stronger and stronger each time the message is repeated. Consequently, being acutely aware of the messages we're sending to our children is critically important.

If you're feeling convicted, like you may have blown it, take heart. It was commonly believed that once our brains are programmed, they are set that way for life. Fortunately, we now know we're able to modify the mental wiring in our brain and how we think!

Through the discovery of "neuroplasticity," we've learned the brain is designed to change its programming. You were most likely taught your brain stops growing new neurons and changing at a very young age.

Because of new medical imaging technology and brain-scanning techniques, we can prove our brain is designed to change throughout our entire lifetime. In fact, your brain is rewiring itself right now!

So, the big questions are:

- How can we rewire our brain to think better?
- How can we be sure the messages we're giving our children are not limiting their success, but cultivating positive thoughts?

To begin, I encourage you to be strategic about the process of first renewing your mind and changing your self-talk. One of the most effective ways to change our programs, and literally rewire our brain is by listening to the right kind of self-talk. Additionally, intentional and focused concentration on positive statements, even for small periods of time during the day, substantially influences our thinking.

As we've learned from the field of neuroscience, the key to rewiring our brain in healthy ways is repetition, repetition, repetition! Repetition is one powerful way the brain gets rewired and gets renewed.

By listening to appropriate, positive self-talk, for ten to twenty minutes a day, you and your children will get appropriate programs, and the proper amount of repetition to rewire your brains in the correct way.

Researchers have discovered that we never get rid of our old programs. They have to be replaced. It was by hearing that the old programs were first put there. Thus, the most effective way for them to be replaced is for us to hear the new ones, repeatedly. A variety of professionally edited and crafted self-talk recordings are available to purchase and listen to for you and your children.

Of course, the messages and the self-talk we're giving to ourselves, and the words we say to our kids, are the most impactful. We want our words to compliment any external self-talk recordings we are using. Mixed messages create confusion.

However, there is one word of caution. Do not give your children false platitudes or fill them with ideas that aren't realistic or are insincere. For example, telling our kids they can be and do anything they want is a noble idea—but it's just not true. Or, telling a child he/she just played a great game, when we both know he/she didn't, does not work. In fact, it has just the opposite effect.

The best way to help our children is to make sure the messages you, the parent, are hearing and the thoughts you're thinking are in your best interest and not based on old, false, negative beliefs. Then, make certain the messages your children are hearing from you and others are setting them up for success.

REFLECTION AND DISCUSSION QUESTIONS:

1. Recall the words you received from your parents. Were they mostly positive or negative and how do you feel this is affecting you still today?
2. What messages are you giving to your children that are not serving them well?

ACTION STEPS:

1. Become intentional about regularly listening to the right kind of self-talk and invest in resources to make sure your children are as well.

2. Become aware of your internal dialogue each day and monitor how much is genuinely positive or negative not based on truth or fact.

BUILD TRUST

Do you trust your children? Do you *want* to trust your children? Trusting our kids can be a challenging proposition. But, if I think back to when I was a child, I can recall telling my parents and siblings things that weren't true, even though I was overall a pretty good kid–at least, I thought so.

No matter how honorable children may be, as I experienced, all children will lie about something at some point. It's part of the human condition that began when sin entered the world, and our kids aren't immune to it. The practical reasons for why kids lie are many and varied. For sure, they want to avoid negative consequences. Additionally, in the moment of deceit, they'll feel it's in their best, most immediate, interest to not be truthful. For them, they may not even consider it as lying, but more like justifying their actions. Does that make their rationale right? No, it doesn't. It just somewhat explains it.

However, if you think about it, do you think our children want us to trust them? If you're not sure, no matter how many times your kids may have disappointed you, the answer is yes. Did you want your parents to trust you, even during times when you were not truthful or trustworthy?

A popular leadership book many businesses have incorporated into their training for key leaders is Patrick Lencioni's exceptional book, *The Five Dysfunctions of a Team*. Not only does the framework he presents apply to companies, but there are many elements he lays out that families can adopt as well. You'll see that the foundational element he begins with is to establish trust. If trust isn't cultivated with the people, then the remaining building blocks needed for the organization to thrive won't be possible.

As parents, it's our responsibility to help our kids learn how to be trustworthy. This doesn't end when our children are out of the home and on their own. A good friend shared how his daughter in her mid-twenties lied to him. She'd somehow gotten a dent in the back of her car. One afternoon she stopped over to his house and he noticed the dent was gone. He asked her how it got fixed. She made up a story that he could tell wasn't the truth. So, he called her out on it. Reluctantly and sheepishly she admitted she'd lied because she basically got swindled into paying way too much to get it fixed, and in her words, she said, "I didn't want you to be disappointed in me." It was then an opportunity, through her tears, to remind her that she can trust him with the truth, and the disappointment is when she's not willing to be truthful.

For us to instill trust, it's important to convey trust initially by what we say and do. It's much more impactful to begin from a place of trust than distrust, even when our kids have messed up, which they will. Our children are more likely to live up to our level of expectation, if it's communicated properly and if they understand what's expected.

If we have a hint of distrust or questioning in our voice when we talk to our children, they will pick up on our doubt or accusation instantly. What's worse is when we accuse them of something they've not done, especially if it's an attack on their character.

Unfortunately, once a lie has been exposed, our natural response may convey we don't really trust our kids or believe they're going to do what we ask. It'll be reflected in our word choice, as well as our tone. Essentially, we're telling our kids we don't believe in them, which is the opposite message we want to send. (Yes, even when they've lied.)

We always want to encourage our kids, expressing we believe in them—that they can and will tell the truth next time, even when there's a price to pay that they may not like. Our challenge is to continue to trust who they are as we simultaneously use their mistakes as an opportunity to teach how important it is to be honest. It's okay for us to point out when trust has been broken; and it can take a period of time for trust to be earned again.

But, if I don't extend trust, no amount of their good behavior will change that. They'll always do something to disappoint, so it will become performance driven relationship very quickly. That's where grace comes in. The same grace I received, I want to extend to my children.

Lastly, consequences for lying will justifiably be part of the equation. Our children ought to understand from the outset that consequences happen for lying, and perhaps even know in advance what those consequences will be.

Believing in our children will foster their desire to excel and live an honorable life. Offering grace when they fail conveys we still believe in them and know they can do better, and that our trust in them is not shaken. No matter how many times they mess up or lie, they need to know we have confidence in them to do the right thing. When we expect them to be honest and trustworthy no matter what, they will be more likely to live up to our wishes.

REFLECTION AND DISCUSSION QUESTIONS:

1. Can you recall a time from your childhood when you lied to your parents or siblings? How were you treated when the lie was exposed?
2. Are you communicating to your children, both by what you say and how you say it, that you believe in them?

ACTION STEPS:

1. If you've not been instilling trust with your children, admit it to them and move forward with renewed expectations, for both them and you.

2. Put in place a system or practice for consequences in the event that your children tell you a lie.

Be Willing to Sacrifice

You probably won't be surprised to hear that parenting requires sacrifices. Prior to having our kids, that concept wasn't something I'd consciously thought about, nor do I recall anyone sharing that tidbit of wisdom with me. So, just in case you haven't already figured it out, I'm sharing that truism with you now: parenting requires sacrifices!

Now, moms will rightly insist that the sacrifices begin well before the baby is born and the parenting begins. Their figure gives way to a noticeable bump and clothes that won't fit anymore. Foods they usually liked are sickening and things they hated they now crave. And many dads have experienced the midnight run to the local convenience store or fast-food place in an effort to placate the craving.

Of course, after the birth is when parents should expect to sacrifice more. Initially, nighttime feedings and fussing means loss of sleep. Doctors' appointments needing to fit into an already busy calendar. Shopping now includes trips to the diaper and baby food aisles. And in case you forgot . . . more laundry . . . picking up toys . . . the bedtime routine . . . tummy aches . . . getting signed up for the best pre-schools . . . and sports teams . .

. packing up to travel . . . and, of course, we have to share all this on social media. With more kids come more sacrifices . . . and more laundry!

In hindsight, those are all relatively minor sacrifices with mostly temporary implications. In my experience, there are more significant sacrifices parents may want to consider, and start to figure out what price they are willing to pay to raise a family that has the best opportunity for success. In most, but not all, cases, these sacrifices will involve our standard definition of success, namely, money or career advancement, and time or personal interests (and often the sacrifices will encompass all of these).

After college and prior to getting married, in addition to running, I'd come to enjoy the sport of golf. I started to play, joined a men's league, and would watch The Golf Channel whenever I could. After Christy and I were married, we moved to Arizona so I could attend Arizona State University in pursuit of my doctoral degree. Even though we lived in a golfing mecca, school and working and lack of money were not conducive to also playing golf.

After getting my degree, we moved to Illinois and I started to golf again and joined a Wednesday night men's league. And then we had our first child . . . and our second two years later and third two years after that. During that time, I'd play in the men's league and try to play on weekends when I could. My love for golf grew. But my uninhibited time to play shrank. The feelings of guilt for not being home to help with the kids diminished my enjoyment of playing. Christy was also working full-time then, so there was an extra burden on her to manage all the kids while I was out playing. You can probably see how that was not conducive for a harmonious marriage.

So, I decided to cut back playing and quit the men's league. After the birth of our fourth child, I only played golf a couple times a year until she was about 13 years old. And, while our older kids took up running as their sport, I believe the Lord blessed my sacrifice and commitment to family by giving me a daughter who, as I mentioned, also developed an interest in golf. Since then, I've been able to share my knowledge and love of golf with her as she learns the game and becomes an accomplished player.

But sacrifices don't only challenge our personal interests. Often, we may have to make career and income sacrifices in order to invest what's needed into our families. After Illinois, we moved to Reno, Nevada where I took a job with a local hospital managing their large fitness/wellness and rehabilitation center. I'd worked there for four years when the non-profit hospital was sold to a for-profit entity. The first year under new ownership our department was left alone, but I could sense a shift in the company culture.

At the time, our four kids were all either in elementary, junior high, or high school. When we moved to Nevada, I'd made a decision that I'd do my best to be home from work before dinner time, so I could help with meal prep and be there for the kids. Of course, they were also involved in other activities and I'd try to be there to watch those, when I could.

Job-wise, our department was running well and I had assembled a very capable team of professionals to work with and assist me. I was then assigned a new VP to oversee our department and he made it known there were advancement opportunities within the hospital.

But what I'd noticed throughout the hospital was that those advancements also came with working long hours, including weekends. Without being given that directive verbally, I knew the expectation even if we were to retain our position . . . but I continued my routine fully aware of the possible outcome. Within nine months, I met with the VP and the HR director and they terminated me without explanation—but we all knew why. I could have chosen to give in and complied with this shift in expectation. But during those years, I knew what was important for my family and, had I acquiesced, I knew I'd regret it.

I've come to believe that even when it doesn't make sense from a worldly perspective, when we stick to our values and honor the commitments we have as husbands and fathers, or wives and mothers, God is faithful and we can trust that he will work out the details, even when we can't see that far down the road. That's certainly been proven true in my life.

Writing this book is another example. Without question, this book would have been completed much, much sooner had it not been for choosing to attend soccer games, track meets, golf matches, and school events, let alone doing household work and helping in the kitchen. Now the book is completed, and I have the satisfaction of knowing I didn't compromise on my values and responsibilities in the process.

One thing to keep in mind as it relates to making sacrifices: don't expect anything in return from your kids. That's not why we're doing it. Of course, when they're young, they'll have no clue about any sacrifice you may be making, whether professionally, personally, or economically. As they get older, they'll start to get it. But please don't use that as an opportunity to hold it over their heads. If you do, you're not really sacrificing, and resentment will overtake your good intentions.

Jesus knew about sacrifice. He gave up his rightful place in heaven to live among us. Ultimately, he gave his life for us, after having lived a perfect life himself. When your children have their own family, they'll mostly likely look back and fully realize how fortunate they were to have parents willing to sacrifice so the family could thrive.

One January, I was asked to give the New Year kick-off keynote for our local Rotary Club. The presentation had the usual smattering of health topics, but I also wanted to get a bit more personal and challenge the members to examine all aspects of their work and home life. At one point, I said, "No amount of success in the business world will make up for a failure at home." What had been a fairly boisterous group suddenly became very quiet. Afterward, many in attendance admitted that sentence resonated with them and they were going to take it to heart.

Will you?

REFLECTION AND DISCUSSION QUESTIONS:

1. What are ways you've sacrificed for your children that cost you advancement or income opportunities, or your personal interests and hobbies?

2. Are there current sacrifices that your conscience is pulling on you to make that you've not yet made?

ACTION STEPS:

1. Identify what possible changes you can make in your priorities that would demonstrate your commitment and make a difference for your family.

2. Ideally, revisit and review these changes quarterly to see what changes you're noticing and what additional changes you can work toward making happen.

CHOOSE YOUR RESPONSE

hildren are generally smart and intuitive, which is beneficial—most of the time. However, all parents have experienced how quickly kids learn to push our buttons. Nevertheless, when we allow the behavior or actions of our children to affect our emotions, then we've succumbed to their wishes. As a result, our children learn how to manipulate us. But that's not what we want, is it?

If you have teenagers, you've probably realized that until kids get through their teen years, they lack mental maturity; their behavior and words can be erratic. Let's face it, kids of most ages don't always make the best choices or do things that serve them well. It's part of maturing, and we need to allow for that process to develop.

But if our kids can tell that their behavior affects our mood, they're more likely to repeat that behavior, even if they don't get what they want. For example, you've no doubt noticed that when children are young and pout, they're attempting to sway our decisions. If we relinquish and comply with their request, it won't be long until they pout again when they don't get their way.

Their influence on our behavior gives them a feeling of control, which is an inherent desire we all share. On the other hand, parents who are afraid they can't manage well, or are insecure about their capabilities, also have the tendency to exert power seeking to gain control. If they don't, it'll feel like they're losing authority or respect.

Ironically, just the opposite happens. Children often respect parents less, and feel more enabled, knowing their behavior can influence how their parents react. If you recognized this as something you've allowed to happen, take heart . . . there is a solution.

To regain your parental position, and not permit your mood or actions to be swayed by your children, recognize and believe in your ability to choose your response to whatever your children do. The better you become at controlling your response, the less influence and control you'll relinquish to your kids . . . and they'll know it and will feel it.

I understand that allowing our children to throw a tantrum without it affecting our emotions is hard, but it is possible. Kids often are unruly and strive to get our attention—to get us to react. But, when we respond appropriately, it'll help extinguish future misbehaviors, because Johnny learns he's not getting the reaction he was seeking.

Not allowing their behavior to influence how we feel doesn't give us cause to ignore them or pretend we don't care. We can still acknowledge what they say and how they feel without it changing our mood. Making a comment to them such as, "I can see that you don't like my decision and I'm sorry about that," affords them the satisfaction of at least knowing they've been heard.

Of course, depending upon the severity of their behavior, how we choose to address their actions will vary. Their conduct may require a consequence or reprimand of some sort. But it's how that penalty is initiated that matters. Do they see our response being cool, calm, and collected, or have our feathers obviously been ruffled?

Have you struggled with allowing the behavior of your children to affect your mood? If you want to change, first become be aware if this is a pattern you've fallen into—how you currently react.

We are responsible for our happiness . . . always! Therefore, we want to develop a high level of self-awareness and emotional intelligence, so we don't react in a negative manner, but respond appropriately. Do you find your emotions or moods are always reflecting your circumstances or the people around you? Are you only happy when your child is behaving (and performing) in a manner you approve of? If so, you may have some work to do. Or, are you already aware of how often your mood is affected by what your kids say or do?

If you feel this is an area for improvement, then you'll need to practice responding versus reacting. Remember, between stimulus and response is our unique ability to choose our response. As I mentioned earlier, anytime we react to what our children say or do, we've handed over the control switch. If we're not intentional in our response, we're allowing them to dictate our emotions. This is true in any relationship. Learning the proper way to respond is a skill we can all develop. But awareness of when and what triggers cause us to respond in a manner that's not in our best interest is crucial. Once aware, we can mentally reframe and imagine those same situations, this time responding peacefully and confidently.

When our kids learn their behavior has minimal impact on how we feel and behave, they'll also learn that we're someone they can trust . . . not manipulate. As a result, it offers them a unique sense of security, and they'll gain respect for us, as well.

You, like me, probably won't always respond perfectly. But by being aware and monitoring your own reaction, you're more likely to consistently communicate in a healthy manner.

REFLECTION AND DISCUSSION QUESTIONS:

1. Monitor your emotions and how you normally behave when your kids do something upsetting. Do you *respond* or *react*?

2. Does their behavior affect how you feel? How long do those feelings last?

ACTION STEPS:

1. If your children's behavior affects how you feel for more than a few minutes, it's an indication you've given up control and a new response pattern will serve you and your children better. Practice responding in a new manner that allows you to maintain your authority and respect.

2. If you've said something hurtful and or need to forgive your kids for something, ask for or give forgiveness now.

PRINCIPLE 25
TALK *TO* YOUR CHILDREN

There is a significant difference between talking *to* our children and talking *at* our children. At first glance, this may not seem to make any sense. But, as you begin to pay attention and listen to yourself talk, if you haven't already, you'll discover the distinction is worth being aware of and making the better choice.

When we're talking *at* our children, our tone will come across as commanding and perhaps dictatorial. Truthfully, when we're in that mode, we probably aren't interested in what they have to say. On the other hand, when we talk *to* our kids, we're talking with them like they're special human beings, instead of objects under our control.

When we talk *to* our children, we're speaking in a style that's much more conversational and relational. Any time we talk *at* them, they'll feel attacked or scolded or like they must defend themselves, which is what will usually happen.

It can be easy for us, as parents, to slip into the habit of talking *at* our children, especially if we have a tendency for wanting to be in control of situations and are set on achieving a desired outcome. In addition to other reasons, it's also how we'll often speak to them when there's too much happening at once and we're feeling overwhelmed or frustrated.

We'll also have the proclivity to speak *at* and not *to* our children when we have a lot of stuff to get done. When that's the case, it's easy to think the drill sergeant method will help us get more done faster, so we start barking orders. Unfortunately, when we address our kids in that manner, they are turned off almost immediately and don't even want to be in our presence, let alone comply.

There may be times when direct, forceful language is necessary, especially if the child is in danger or making a foolish choice. But, if speaking to your children that way has become the norm, then change is in order. We want to err on the side of our dialogue being more relational and not simply transactional. Our goal is to reel them into our conversation when we want to talk or have a request of them, not repel them.

If you feel that you've developed the habit of primarily talking *at* your children, what changes can you initiate so that you'll begin speaking *to* or *with* them? You'll find that when you approach your interactions with this mindset, you'll actually enjoy your conversations much more, instead of dreading the conflict that is otherwise likely to ensue.

It may seem like a slight distinction at first. But, as you listen to yourself talk, the style you've developed will surface. Now that you're aware of it, you'll be able to change your approach and, as a result, transform your relationship.

REFLECTION AND DISCUSSION QUESTIONS:

1. Assess how you currently communicate with your children . . . do you primarily talk *at* them or *to* them?

2. If you feel that you've developed the habit of primarily talking *at* your children, what changes can you initiate so that you'll begin speaking *to* or with them?

ACTION STEPS:

1. Ask your spouse what he or she thinks about how you currently talk to your children. What does your spouse hear when you talk to the kids? Is it different for each child?

2. Become intentional about talking to your children instead of talking at your kids.

PRINCIPLE 26
say yes

Think back to when you were a kid growing up. Do you recall how your requests were generally met from your parents or those in authority? How about this . . . when you asked for something, what were you hoping your parents or guardians would say? If I'm right, I'm guessing you wanted them to say, "yes!"

Now unless you've done a 180, chances are that if your requests as a kid were usually met with "no," you probably have a tendency to respond to your kids with the same response. But, does saying "no" more than "yes" make you a better parent? In working with parents, it's been my experience that most aren't even cognizant of how often they say "yes" or "no." But if we asked their kids, I bet they'd have a quick response.

Our children ask things of us for a variety of reasons. Maybe they can't find their socks, or want something to eat, or perhaps they want to have a friend over. But the questions we want to pay special attention to are any that require our involvement, or something that would give them much joy, even if they don't need our participation. Those are the questions we want to say "yes" to.

That's the spirit behind the Netflix movie, *"Yes Day,"* if you've not seen it. In viewing the movie, it struck me how many times in the past, as our kids were growing, that I missed wonderful opportunities to say, "Yes." I don't need to give you all the excuses I probably used to say, "No," or, "Not now," but in hindsight I wished I'd have said, "Yes" more often. Most of the time, a yes won't have cost me anything other than my time and energy, or some sleep.

As a young kid, I loved western movies. I recall one evening a western came on after the 10:00 p.m. news and I'd started watching it. After about five minutes, my dad came in and saw I was watching it. Anticipating the answer would be a no, I was surprised (and delighted) when he said I could watch a bit longer. Although it didn't happen often, this night he sat down and started watching with me . . . until the end, which was way past my bedtime. Did that create an impression on me? Well, I don't remember most nights at home, but I remember that one.

As Jim Daly, President of Focus on the Family, said, "It's the wise parent who looks for opportunities to say "yes" to their child's requests. And I get it; most parents are just trying to keep the family's train on the tracks. Shaking up a routine or surrendering a weekend might not be at the top of your list. The request might seem inconvenient or even make you a little nervous. But think again. Take the long view. I'd like to challenge you to find reasons to say "yes" to your sons and daughters. I suspect you won't regret it."

In the movie *"Yes Day,"* the family of five agrees to a day where the mother and father consent to whatever the kids want for a day. I'd agree that's extreme, but the movie is to entertain and emit laughs. Of course, parents who let their kids do everything they want are headed down the wrong tracks, just as is the family where the parents say "no" to most everything.

As you know, there are always times when a definite no is the necessary response. But take time to assess and reflect, as you seek for a reason and a way to say, "Yes." If you're extremely risk adverse, step back and be sure you're being realistic about what could happen and not squashing their fun because of your fears or dislikes.

One Sunday, we'd received a pile of snow and it was still coming down and winds were whipping at 27 mph. After talking to some of her friends, my teenage daughter came down excitedly to tell us that they'd decided to go sledding right after church. Did they not realize it felt like 13 degrees outside and the roads hadn't been plowed? Because I hate the cold, what do you think my internal decision was? But after quick reflection, verbally I said, "Yes, if we can get there safely." She was good with that answer and it maintained her enthusiasm and excitement as she anticipated a fun time sledding with her friends. The cold and snow was my concern, not hers. Was there risk? Sure. She could have been injured sledding or gotten frost bite, or we could have gotten stuck trying to get there. But, I'd rather our kids be willing to get out and try things than be sheltered and fearful of what might happen.

But what if one parent is predictably a "yes" parent and the other a "no"? Of course, our kids will figure that out and use that to their advantage. A unified front is always the best way to go into battle. So, parents will find that, when possible, consulting with each other in private before answering will prevent lots of conflict between each other and with their kids.

Looking for opportunities to say "yes" as a family or one-one-one with a child can be pretty incredible. As a parent, seek to find that loving balance between your yeses and your nos. In doing so, you'll create a home environment that your kids will enjoy growing up in, because they'll enjoy being with you while still respecting the boundaries you've created.

When it was time to sled, the weather got worse. So, my daughter understood when I told her I wasn't willing to drive her to go sledding with her friends. But, I offered to go sledding with her at a spot we could walk to from our house. In this case, I had to say "no" to driving her, but "yes" to sledding.

Reflection and Discussion Questions:

1. Reflect and discuss what you experienced growing up—were your requests met with affirmation or denials?
2. What are some recent examples you can recall when you could have said yes to your kids, but said no instead?

Action Steps:

1. For the next few days, pay attention and keep track of what your natural response is when your kids ask something that involves you. After your observation time, intentionally respond with a "yes" answer that will surprise and delight your kids.

Pause and Consider Before Responding

As we established, it goes without saying that we can't and won't do everything our children want or give them everything they ask for. At least, I hope that's the case, if we want healthy kids.

However, when our children ask to do something or ask for something, they have a reason for asking. At the time, we may think it's silly, or illogical, or nonsensical, but what we think doesn't really matter. How we respond does matter . . . a lot.

The point is this: when our children ask something, let's pause long enough to sincerely reflect, and then respond in a manner that gives them the satisfaction of knowing we're at least considering their request. As is the case for everyone, they want to know that they matter and that their opinion counts. They want to feel validated. Our children are no different than us in that regard.

Anytime we nonchalantly, or too quickly, dismiss their requests, we've invalidated our children. Alternatively, we extend and demonstrate respect by letting them know we've heard their requests and have considered them, even if the answer is going to be, "No," or, "Not now." In addition to our reply, we're well served by taking a moment to offer a brief, meaningful reason for our answer. They may not like the response, but at least they'll have satisfaction and contentment knowing we've listened, understood, and considered their request.

Now comes the more challenging part. If they start to complain or try to negotiate, it's important that we stand firm in our decision (almost always). When the pushback continues, the goal is to simply restate firmly, with love, that we've heard their request and have thought about it, but the answer is still "No." Of course, to the best of your ability, conveying our answer in a clear, calm, and collected manner underscores our resolve.

If your children never take "No" for an answer, it's most likely because too often you've given in to their repeated requests. They know, if they're persistent enough, you'll wear down and they'll get their way.

That's why it's vitally important to stop and think before you answer, to perceptibly consider the request, so you can have integrity and stand firm in your decisions. If your response comes without thought, and you then change your mind, you've just reinforced the behavior you don't want your kids to learn.

When you establish a habit of pausing and considering before responding, you'll all feel better about the conversations, there'll be less conflict, and the relationship will remain connected.

REFLECTION AND DISCUSSION QUESTIONS:

1. When your children ask for something, what is your initial response? Is it thoughtful or predetermined?

2. Do your children get frustrated often with your responses or do they attempt to negotiate incessantly?

ACTION STEPS:

1. Surprise your kids by giving them a response that is out of character with how you've primarily responded.
2. Practice pausing and considering prior to giving your response, and pay attention to the changes you notice over time.

PRINCIPLE 28
PAY ATTENTION TO YOUR TONE

Y ou've probably heard the adage, "It's not what you say . . . it's how you say it that matters." That may sound cliché, but it's also sound advice. And, if we apply it to our parenting, we'll reap the rewards.

Well-known author and clinical psychologist Dr. Henry Cloud said, "Your heart will reveal itself in your tone . . . no matter what the words say. People will respond to tone more than words." When we say something to our children and they ignore us or respond in a manner that seems defensive or disrespectful, instead of reacting critically toward them, it's better to reflect on how we said what we said. We can say the exact same words, or make the exact same request of our children, and get a completely different response depending upon how we come across.

If our kids sense there's love and caring behind our words, they'll be much more apt to respond likewise. But, if our words are harsh or critical or condemning in tone, then they'll likely reply in a defensive manner, which will elevate conflict. Which is the better outcome?

Our words, depending on how we say them, can aggravate our children more than most anything. Here is what I've found to be true: 10 percent of conflict in relationships is due to difference of opinion and 90 percent is due to wrong tone of voice. If that's even half right, just think of how much conflict can be avoided!

One strategy that helped increase my awareness was to record myself. Using my smartphone, it was easy to do. All I did was lay it on the counter and hit record any time they came home from school, or during a meal, or whenever I normally interacted with them. Then I played the recording in private, paying special attention to my tone. Unfortunately, what I heard wasn't always very flattering.

Of course, we want to continually be aware of our spoken words. But even more important is our tone. It's always the responsibility of the person speaking to talk in a manner that will be received as intended. It's never right to put the burden on the listener to reinterpret or decode what we're trying to say. Keep in mind, what compliments or detracts from our words and tone of voice are our eyes. Our eyes often reveal what we're really thinking or how we feel, in spite of what we say. Practice looking at yourself in the mirror with you talk and see what others are seeing.

When we're able to deliver a message in the same way we like to be addressed, we'll have a healthier exchange. And our children will respond better because they'll feel like we care, which of course we do.

REFLECTION AND DISCUSSION QUESTION:

1. What kind of tone do you prefer others to speak to you in? How do you react when you perceive others are using a negative tone (e.g., irritated, condescending, judgmental, etc.)

2. Reflect. What was the tone like in the home you grew up in? Is your current tone like what you heard from your parents?

ACTION STEPS:

1. Ask other family members (maybe your spouse or your older kids) what they think of your tone. How do they describe it?

2. Pay attention to how you speak to each child. Do you use the same tone generally for them all or do you use a different tone with each child? If so, why is that?

DON'T PLAY THE BLAME GAME

You've probably concluded by now that wisely choosing the words we say and how we say them is a central point for us to remember. A big red flag is when we say something to our children (or our spouse) that comes across as blaming or accusing. If you've done this, most likely you've experienced your children becoming defensive in response.

If we're not careful, blaming can become a nasty habit. When we blame, it's really an attempt to avoid taking responsibility or an errant effort to persuade our kids to change their behavior. Plus, when we blame, we're teaching our children to do the same thing—blame and make excuses for their behavior.

Our children witness us blaming whenever they hear us complain or make excuses for anything that's going on in our life, as well as when we directly blame them. When they hear us blame someone else or our employer or the government or the weather, they quickly learn to do the same. And when we blame them directly, we'll assuredly activate their defensive response, as was mentioned previously.

Plus, have you ever placed blame on your children only to find out you were wrong? If false accusations are done repeatedly, there is no overstating the damage it can do to the psyche of their young impressionable minds. In addition, it's sending the message we don't have confidence in or trust them. There is nothing children want more than to know we believe in them (more on this in the next principle). But if we are repeatedly blaming them or falsely accusing them, eventually they'll quit trying altogether.

It's your choice to set the example and become aware of any time you tend to blame. First, become aware and catch yourself and stop blaming immediately. When you fall into the habit, recognize the behavior and then apologize to your children for the slip-up. We don't want our children to catch us being hypocritical in this area. So, we never want to admonish our kids for blaming or making excuses and then let them hear us blame someone or make excuses about something else.

Here's a relevant quote from Dr. Wayne Dyer, who stated, "All blame is a waste of time. No matter how much fault you find with another, and regardless of how much you blame him, it will not change you. The only thing blame does is to keep the focus off you when you are looking for external reasons to explain your unhappiness or frustration. You may succeed in making another feel guilty about something by blaming him, but you won't succeed in changing whatever it is about you that is making you unhappy."

When we accept 100 percent responsibility, not for what happens to us but for how we respond, we're modeling behavior that our children need to see. Soon they'll start to follow suit, which will put them on the best path for life.

REFLECTION AND DISCUSSION QUESTIONS:

1. How often do you find yourself placing blame on your children or on others? Take note, as you may not be aware you're in the habit of blaming.

2. What is the reaction from your children when you do place blame on them?

ACTION STEPS:

1. Try and catch yourself before you blame, and re-word what you're saying so it doesn't come across as blaming.
2. When you catch yourself blaming your kids or spouse, immediately apologize with sincerity.

PRINCIPLE 30
EXPECT THE BEST

At times, I'm sure it's hard to believe this: our children really do want to please us. Have you ever thought about that? Do you really believe it? Think about when you were growing up. Did you want to please your parents? Believing that our kids want to please us will shape our prevailing demeanor and attitude toward our children.

In his book *The Happiness Advantage*, Shawn Achor states, "What we expect from people (and from ourselves) manifests itself in the words we use, and those words can have a powerful effect on the end results." Our children sense when we're for them, or if we doubt them, their ability, and even their worth. It's important to know that, inherently, they're wired to want to please us and do what's right. Even though they are surprisingly resilient, if they feel that no matter what they do they'll never please us, at some point they'll quit trying.

This is a good place to reemphasize the 5:1 ratio. Even a little criticism, condemnation, or continual correction outweighs praise and acknowledgement in the minds of our children. So, we might think we're doing a good job if we've established the pattern of being intentional in giving positive feedback. But, if we're falling short of dishing out significantly more positive recognition than negative feedback, in our kids' minds, we'll be perceived as always being negative.

Our children need to know we are for them. We want to be their best cheerleader and encourager. That's not to suggest we lose sight of reality in our feedback and discipline. But what we look for usually appears, and what we focus on grows. If we're looking for things our kids do well or that we appreciate, we're more likely to see and recognize and acknowledge it. If we're primarily focusing on what our kids do wrong, then that's what we'll notice.

For some parents, depending on their personality and past experiences, dishing out positive encouragement and praise may be a challenge. Chances are, if you never received encouragement or affirmations from your parents as a youngster, and if they were focused on what you did wrong, instead of expecting the best from you, you're likely to repeat that mistake as a parent. Here's encouragement for you to be intentional about not continuing that cycle in your home.

From the work of Dr. Gary Chapman and his book, *The Five Love Languages*, many of us have already learned about the key ways that each of us like to be treated, including our kids. Basically, *The Five Love Languages* helps identify how a person best gives and receives love, via one or more of five "languages": giving, service, quality time, physical touch, and words of encouragement. Perhaps you already know if words of affirmation are an important love language for your kids. If not, I encourage you to use Dr. Chapman's material to review and identify how your kids are wired and what's important to them.

If beginning to expect the best and affirming your kids is a growth area for you, start small and build on each opportunity interact with your children. You can expect the best out of them (even in the midst of failures) and become known as an encourager . . . the encourager your children need you to be.

As the parents, we set the tone for what our home feels like. Whatever tone or mood we establish will permeate through the walls of our home and impact how our kids react, feel, and behave. How do you want your home to feel?

> *"If you want to get the best out of a person*
> *you must look for the best that is in him."*
> - Bernard Haldane

REFLECTION AND DISCUSSION QUESTIONS:

1. How has the home you grew up in and the feedback you received from your parents—positive or negative—affected how you parent now?

2. If there are reasons you're hesitant to expect the best from your kids and be an encourager, what are they?

ACTION STEPS:

1. Every day, regardless of their ages, affirm something your kids have done, no matter how trivial it may seem. The more you do this, the more you'll notice to affirm.

2. If you haven't, complete the *Five Love Languages* assessment for each of your kids and discuss what you've learned. Based on your findings, what can you do differently?

PRINCIPLE 31

KEEP PERSPECTIVE

Have you ever made a subjective, over-inflated comment, trying to motivate your child to action? We've likely all done it. For example, your child comes home from school and makes himself a snack. After he finishes eating, he leaves a few items on the previously spotless kitchen counter and heads to his room. You come home and find some food still out and dishes scattered on the counter. You yell, "Who made this big mess in here?"

Now, let's be honest. Is it *really* a big mess, or could the counter be cleaned up in less than a few minutes? And when these scenarios play out, it leads to unnecessary contention and conflict.

We tend to react relative to our expectations. If we expect that at no time will there be any clothing or books on the bedroom floor and everything will always be in order, then any time we open the door and see a few items lying around, we may perceive it as a huge mess. But is that factually true? Is it a huge mess, or could those few items be quickly put away?

When reality does not match our words or our reaction, our children will learn to discount what we say. Does the boy who cried wolf story come to mind? When we exaggerate, it not only fails to make an impact on our children; it actually has the opposite of its intended effect! To them, it's obvious our spoken words don't match reality, at least not in their eyes. Projecting how we *feel* about something we *see* seldom transfers to how our kids see it. We see things through a different lens than our children do.

One good way to move away from this model of communication is to avoid using terms like *never* and *always* when we speak to our children. How often does anything *always* happen, unless we're talking about the sun coming up in the morning? However, it's easy, without thinking, to spout out that our kids are "always" late or "never" finish their homework. But how often is that truly the case? It's better we refrain from using terms and word choices that are an exaggeration.

When we speak truthfully to our kids, they learn they can trust us. When we exaggerate, they know we're blowing smoke. Once it clears, everything looks differently. Our goal is to establish the habit of seeing things the way they really are, and then expressing it in a manner that reflects reality. Doing so enhances their desire to take appropriate action.

Children react much more positively when we don't overreact but communicate in a relatable manner. They'll feel more secure because instincts will tell them we're more in touch with reality. As a result, learning will increase and their responses to our instruction will be more favorable.

Reflection and Discussion Questions:

1. How often do you find yourself saying "you always" or "you never" when you communicate?

2. What are the hot buttons that tend to set you off and lead to conflict?

Action Steps:

1. Identify situations when you might tend to exaggerate or overblow things.

2. Think about what really matters. What things are making you upset that really don't make that big of a difference? Now, only pick the battles worth fighting.

SEEK TO BUILD UP

A s parents, we automatically assume the mantle of authority. It's our anointed position simply by being a father or mother. The question is, even though we have authority, do we harness our influence positively, and embody and display the traits of leadership?

Authority and leadership are not synonymous. Popular leadership and management author, Ken Blanchard, said, "The key to successful leadership is influence, not authority." A dictator can have authority without demonstrating leadership.

The term "leadership" implies having a positive influence on those we lead. We properly use our position of influence when we boost those under our authority. As leaders, we strive to always have the best interests of those we lead as a top priority.

It's important to acknowledge that our position of authority as a parent is used to either build up our children or to tear them down. The words we speak (both what we say and how we say it) to our children have the greatest impact on whether we are building them up or tearing them down. Think of it as "The Elevator Principle" . . . we're either lifting those around us up, or letting them down.

However, building up should never be done insincerely. Kids will see through that. They know instinctively if what is being said to them is genuine, earnest, and meaningful or if the words are just false praise.

We are instructed in how we are to speak in Ephesians 4:29, which says, "Do not let any unwholesome talk come out of your mouth, but only that which is helpful for building others up according to their needs that it may benefit those who listen." That includes when and how we talk to our children. What God wants us to do is to show faith in our kids, so they can believe what He says about them.

True leaders—those who are respected—apply this principle because they understand what leaders are called to do. We want everything we say and do to come from a spirit of teaching, instructing, coaching, correcting, and encouraging, and not criticizing, condemning, judging, or discouraging.

No doubt, you'll mess up. I know I do. We're human. And with our humanity, our emotions will take over and we'll fail to do what we know is best. But that's simply a time to recognize, reflect, redirect, and rebuild, because the next opportunity to have a positive impact will probably be coming toward you soon.

Reflection and Discussion Questions:

1. In what ways may you be unintentionally tearing down your children when you talk?
2. What changes can you make to become more of a coach and less of a critic?

Action Steps:

1. Make sure the feedback you're giving is authentic and genuine and not done just to make your children feel good in the moment.
2. Implement changes you can make to become more of a coach and less of a critic.

BE DISCIPLINED IN YOUR DISCIPLINE

Have you ever observed a child behaving in a way that challenges the parent, testing to see if the dad or mom is really paying attention or really cares? Kids push boundaries intentionally hoping we'll step in and draw the line. How we respond to these challenges speaks volumes into the worth of our children.

When we discipline our children, we still want our words and actions to be done in a manner that builds them up, as was previously mentioned. The simplest formula to follow, in order to be consistent, is outlined in the book by Ken Blanchard, *The One Minute Manager*. The process flows as follows:

- First, say something affirming to your child.
- Second, explain what was done wrong and why it was wrong.
- Third, express your love for who your child is and impart confidence that he can do better.

What's critically important when correcting our children is our emotional state, which will be clearly conveyed in how we deliver our correction. Although difficult, remaining about our wits in these situations is the best strategy. Advantages include thinking more creatively and being more objective because we're in a calm versus a hyper state of mind. In addition to thinking better, we'll act more mature and feel more positive about the outcome. By remaining composed, we're sending a message to them that their behavior isn't going to trigger or control our behavior.

As you probably know, how you approach discipline is setting an example for your children. How you do what you do carries more weight than what you've done to correct the wrong. For your children, their first impression of God is what they see in you. A good question to ask yourself is, "Am I reflecting God's character in the way I discipline and interact with my children?"

Being willing to discipline is what we are called to do, and we're instructed how to do it. Ephesians 6:4, says, "And now a word to you fathers. Don't make your children angry by the way you treat them. Rather, bring them up with the discipline and instruction approved by the Lord." To reiterate, more than what we say, it's the way we treat our children, especially as we discipline, that will determine how they'll respond in the short term. But more importantly, our actions will also chart the course for how they will discipline our grandchildren in the future.

My friend, Chris, shared a story with me about his teenage years and a specific incident with his father that still, as a grown man, brings him to tears. His father was an imposing 263-pound retired Chicago Bears lineman and unafraid to vocally express his emotions. As Chris recalled, he was not the best of kids and caused his parents many sleepless nights. The incident involved being suspended from high school and anxiously waiting for the backlash when his dad picked him up. But, to Chris' surprise, his dad headed to the Burger King drive-through and then went to a park where he used to coach Chris in soccer. As Chris states, "Instead of yelling and threatening me, we talked. And while I knew I had made a big-time mistake, in that moment I knew all 6'3" of my dad loved me. That moment had a greater impact on me, my relationship with him, and my memory of his spirit, than any other moment in my childhood. I think that God does the very same thing: sometimes shedding a tear as we make mistakes, and other times tearing up with joy as we do what pleases Him."

Because we have experience, knowledge, and wisdom, we're able to see what our kids can't see, yet. We'll most likely be right, if we've taken the time to understand the dynamics of the situation. But, even if we're right, we're wrong if we're rude or demeaning in our approach.

With the delicate nature of discipline, don't lose opportunities to teach and instruct because we've lost their respect due to how we handled the situation. At the same time, we still want them to understand and revere the authoritative nature of our fatherhood or motherhood. Such is the balancing act of parenting.

When we set boundaries and establish effective discipline, we're at our best as a parent. When we're consistent in our approach and delivery, we create a healthy environment for our kids to grow and flourish.

Reflection and Discussion Questions:

1. How would you describe your method of discipline? How do you think your children would describe your method of discipline?
2. Are you reflecting God's character in the way you discipline? Why or why not?

Action Steps:

1. Identify one change you could make in your discipline that would make the biggest positive difference and implement that change.
2. Rehearse and practice the *One Minute Manager* method described in this chapter.

Make These Investments

Have you ever wondered how children can be so different? Have you ever bought something because one child loved it, but another would never even touch it? If you have more than one child, you've probably recognized that no two children are the same. The degree of difference can be mild or extreme.

One often overlooked factor affecting our kid's tendencies is birth order. There is published literature available to explain the impact that birth order can have on shaping the personality and characteristics of children, if you're interested. In addition to birth order, experiences they have at school, in sports, with their peers, and at home also impact how they behave.

As parents, we want to make investments in our children that will continue to grow for a lifetime. When we consider the various stages of life our kids go through, it quickly becomes apparent that we only have a few short years to effectively influence or invest in our children. So, what can we do to positively influence their growth, development, and future? Here are five fundamental investments we can make while they're in our home that will yield positive dividends.

1. **Discover and detect.** Underlying all our children's unique qualities is the "shape" that each child has been given. One responsibility we have as parents is to be a detective . . . discovering the unique gifting and strengths of our children. The instruction provided in Proverbs 22:6 says, "Train up a child in the way he should go, and when he is old he will not depart from it." The verse implies that we are to help them develop in the way they are bent, which means their natural giftings, tendencies, and passions. Questions we can ask to help in our discovery include:
   - What are their natural strengths and weaknesses?
   - How are they gifted?
   - What skills do they possess?
   - What do they naturally gravitate toward?
   - What energizes them?

By asking these types of questions and observing what they do and listening to what they say, we'll find clues. With those in hand, it becomes much easier and clearer to discern the direction in which to point and guide them.

2. **Become involved.** To understand their bent, it's important to become involved enough with our children to figure out what makes them tick. As they mature and their bent continually unfolds, our role is to lead them along that path and allow them to grow more fully in those areas. That doesn't happen unless we're investing time and interacting with them to learn who they are and how they were created.

You've heard the ongoing debate regarding whether quality or quantity of time with kids is more important. Instead of debating, just ask your kids. I really don't think there is much of a debate. You'll quickly find out that children of all ages spell love "T-I-M-E." Our goal is to strive for as much time that is of high quality with our kids as we can create. Obviously, the more kids we have, the more difficult it is to spend large amounts of quality time with each one.

If that's the case, it's important to be intentional and know when those opportunities are during the week, so we can unplug from our world and plug into theirs. As they get older and more involved with school, activities, and friends, there's usually even less time to spend with them.

But, when we're committed to investing time with them and involving ourselves in their lives, we'll create an environment that fosters enthusiasm, engagement, and excitement. As a result, their level of self-worth and confidence grows.

3. **Guide and coach.** While being led along the path of self-discovery, our children benefit greatly from our guidance and direction. In addition to being their parent, adopting the mindset of also being their coach complements parenting very well.

If you've ever had a coach, ask yourself, "What behaviors did my best coaches display?" In reflecting on those who coached me, the most effective coaches believed in me, were encouraging, respectful, inspiring, affirming, corrected not criticized, built up, focused on the positives, and disciplined with love.

When we model the best characteristics of a coach, not only do our children benefit, but we'll also receive immeasurable joy in watching their growth, development, and contribution. We're preparing them for the world that awaits. When they enter the work world, we'll pray they work for a manager who's also a great coach.

4. **Acknowledge and accept**. Sometimes our child's bent will closely match our own skills and interests. But sometimes we wonder

whose child this is because their interests and giftings don't remotely resemble ours. Our challenge is not to judge or change their bent, but to shape and nurture the way God created them.

Since each child is unique, and most likely different than their siblings, being critical or comparing our children is never desirable. They are best served when we accept their distinctions and never judge one against the other. God knew what he was doing. That was his job. It's not ours. When we accept and then guide them along their path, we'll also experience much less conflict as we journey together. However, if we can see the path they are on is leading them in a direction that is not in their best interest, our task is to figure out what we need to do to redirect their journey.

Another benefit of having children with differences is that their uniqueness makes each of them stronger and enhances their growth. As they live with and witness the uniqueness between each other (as well as between the parents), it forces them to learn adaptation skills. Having those experiences will boost their ability to integrate and adjust to the differences they'll face in the real world.

5. **Be transformed.** Before we start lamenting and wishing our children were more alike to make parenting easier, consider this benefit. Because they are different, we're pushed to grow and develop our character. For example, because each of our four children are unique, I've had to learn more about myself and figure out how I need to change and grow in order to more effectively parent. One realization I had was that the quirks in my children that bothered me the most also exposed how and where I needed to change.

That didn't happen by accident. The question is—am I taking advantage of this living laboratory while they are in my presence? This is my time to learn and grow to become more like Christ and the person I was created to be. Chances are that if I'm wishing they were different, so it's less challenging for me, I'm missing out on the greatest opportunity I have to become transformed.

As we learn our children's bent, we're investing time, energy, and resources to help them along this journey. You invest in those things or people that we want to grow, just like we invest your money hoping that it grows. When our children sense we're committed and plugged into their world, not only do we enhance their strengths, but our effort also boosts our relationship with them. And that's a pretty good investment!

ReFLeCTION anD DISCUSSION QUeSTIONS:

1. Of the five fundamentals listed, which are you excelling in and which areas have the most room for growth?
2. How do you feel about the amount and quality of time you spend with each child?

ACTION STePS:

1. Review and answer each of the five questions for each child in the "Discover and Detect" section above.
2. Focus on one fundamental this week and identify how you can make positive changes in that area.

PRINCIPLE 35
KNOW YOURSELF

How well do you know yourself? Well, just let me say, the better you know yourself, the less likely you are to become frustrated, discouraged, and disappointed. Knowing your natural tendencies, your strengths and weaknesses, your triggers, and your personality traits will put you in the best position to develop deep, abiding relationships with your spouse and kids, and achieve greater levels of success in all areas of life.

I know some people will respond to this concept by thinking that I am the way I am and nothing is going to change that. Which is true, if there's no desire to receive feedback or make things better. But, in reality, we're not in a fixed state, but are moldable and capable of making positive changes, which will make life better, resolve or minimize unnecessary conflict and confusion as we communicate, and lead to more fulfilling and enjoyable interactions with everyone—including our kids.

To kick off this journey of exploring yourself, start by becoming aware and noticing your emotional status throughout the day. Pay attention to when you are naturally up or down, energized or drained, and available or unavailable for emotional engagement or interaction.

What are the times or situations, or the day parts, when you need to have your guard up, so you don't get into situations or say things you later regret? Is your worst time in the morning or evening? I know, for example, the time of day when I have the least patience is right before bedtime . . . I'm tired and my pillow is calling.

Knowing our hot buttons enables us to pay attention to our reactive behavior. If you know, for example, you're generally tired and lacking energy at the end of the day, try to be more conscious and intentional about being patient and not engaging in conversations or tasks that will require of you what you cannot give.

Knowing yourself basically involves setting personal boundaries to insulate yourself and protect your kids from unnecessary conflict. Most people are usually not at their best when they are either hungry or tired or trying to do too many things. Knowing yourself also allows you to structure your day or week in a manner that makes you most productive, and least likely to engage in behavior you later regret.

A potentially eye-opening awareness exercise is to pretend Jesus is physically in the room with you. Do you like what He is seeing in you? If not, why not? What can you change and how can you show up differently next time, so He'd say, "Well done," to what He's observed?

Self-awareness, which is directly related to knowing yourself and discussed further in the next section, is a never-ending process. It's critical for how we get along in the world and in forming the relationships we have with our children. There's abundant information about emotional intelligence already in print. If this is an area you'd like to further improve, investing in a book about emotional intelligence will help both you and your children develop these valuable skills.

In addition, there are many tools at our fingertips that can help us to learn more about ourselves, our spouse, and our kids, which can be very helpful in establishing better communication and enhance our relationships. If you're not familiar with these, look up some common assessments like DISC, *Leading from Your Strengths*, The Enneagram, *Strengths Finder*, or The Fascinate Test. If you do a web search, you'll discover many others.

Each of these tools can help you learn more about yourself, how you best communicate, your strengths and weaknesses, your natural tendencies, and how to work more effectively within a work or family unit. I've utilized several of these insightful tools and our family all completed The Fascinate Test and The Enneagram.

Once you complete the assessment, you can utilize the information by engaging your family in discussions based on the report that is generated. From there, use those discussions as a springboard for personal growth that will someday extend into helping your kids in their professional career paths. We were able to laugh at how well the tools pinpointed who we were, our similarities and differences, and then have fun exploring how we could grow and communicate better with each other.

God made each of us unique . . . He made us on purpose—for a purpose. Our responsibility is to discover who we are and how we can unleash the unlimited potential we possess. Learning about yourself . . . how you're wired and how each of your kids are wired . . . will help you in your relationships with each other, and in pursuing your passions.

REFLECTION AND DISCUSSION QUESTIONS:

1. How well do you know yourself? Would you consider yourself "self-aware"?

2. Based on what you're learning about yourself, what do think you either need to do or avoid doing in order to relate/respond better to your children?

ACTION STEPS:

1. Identify your best times of the day and the worst times of your day. Work to plan your appropriate activities with your children according to what you identify.

2. If you haven't, select one of the assessment tools that is most appropriate for you and your spouse and kids (if they are old enough) to take. After you've completed it, review each of your reports with each other. Discuss what you've learned and some changes you can make moving forward that will help how you communicate with each other.

OBSERVE YOURSELF

Have you ever tried to step outside of yourself and observe your behavior? If you saw the movie *Ghost,* remember that it depicted the lead actor, played by Patrick Swayze, having died, but after his death he could hover over and observe the lead female role, played by Demi Moore. A strange concept, to be sure, but the difference here is that you're outside looking down and observing your *own* self. What would you see?

Engaging in this unique technique requires the skill of self-awareness. This simply means, you—in the moment—are in a present enough state of mind to become an observer of your thoughts, words, and actions . . . and the results they are producing. Another closely related term is mindfulness.

We humans are creatures of habit. It's easy to fall into unhealthy patterns of thought and action, which are revealed in the words we say and the tone we use. However, it's not as easy to become aware of those words and tone. So, it's a worthwhile exercise to step back and assess if your behavior aligns with who you desire to be—your best self!

To expedite the self-awareness process, I encourage you to identify and write down the best parental attributes you wish to demonstrate. Most people come up with virtues like caring, compassionate, patient, encouraging, honest, kind, fun, engaged, present, etc. What words are on *your* list?

Now, the next time you interact with your children, for five minutes, allow your mind to hover above the room, observing the exchanges taking place between you and them. How do you look—what's the expression on your face? How do you come across? How do your words sound? How attentive are you? Are you listening well? Are you noticing your child's mood and non-verbal cues? Overall, how did the interaction go and what was the result? Did the conversation end positively and build the relationship . . . or something less?

It's up to us to decide how we want to behave within our homes. We're responsible for how we show up in every situation, whether at home or in the work world or at the grocery store. In that regard, our home becomes our testing and proving ground for how we will interact with the rest of the world.

It's similar when someone visits our home. Does our behavior and how we talk to our children change when someone else is in the room? If it does, it's an indication that our normal communication to our children is not our best, and likely not building them up. If it were, why would we change when others are observing us?

Practicing the skill of self-awareness and becoming an observer of ourselves enables us to be in tune with how we're coming across to our children. And in doing so, we'll detect if our behavior reflects what we desire it to be.

Practicing this skill may be difficult at first, especially during times when emotions run high. But with practice, your self-awareness will improve, and you'll enjoy more success in being the person you really want to be—and likely find much more joy in being a parent.

REFLECTION AND DISCUSSION QUESTIONS:

1. What are the best parenting qualities that you aspire to possess and display?

2. What appeals to you about growing in self-awareness? What makes you hesitate?

ACTION STEPS:

1. For five minutes, pretend you are hovering above the room observing yourself interact with your children. What do you observe?

2. What changes do you notice that you could make today?

Be Ready To Engage

You've just settled down to check in with your friends on Facebook, or watch your favorite TV show, or snuggle into bed to read your book. The door opens—and your solitude is suddenly shattered! Your child needs your attention, or your help. Has that ever happened to you? With four kids, it was a regular occurrence in our house.

So, how do you respond? Do you snap or smile? Do you grimace or are you gracious? Do you ignore her or engage? Does she get the impression she is a bother and burden . . . or a blessing? What is the impression you want her to have?

Our response, in these and similar situations, shapes the relationship we are forming with our children. The self-worth our children are developing is also influenced in the process. Whether we're always conscious of it or not, the true nature of a child is to please us—the parents. Anytime our children feel like they're not pleasing to us, an imprint is left in their souls. The more often that impression is given, the deeper the mark.

Establishing the pattern of being receptive to our kids' interruptions, instead of making them feel like they are a burden or a bother, will provide dividends when they want to talk about something bigger than just finding their socks. By reacting properly to the small things, we're preparing the pathway for future discussions that will be of more significance, like relationship problems or other life issues they will undoubtedly encounter.

Of course, we also want to set proper boundaries, so we're able to get things done, or relax, or spend uninterrupted time with our spouse. It's our responsibility to let them know ahead of time if we'll be busy and don't want to be interrupted. In those situations, we need to make clear how long it will be, and when we'll be back "on duty." Otherwise, in their mind, we're available and ready for engagement . . . and that's really what we want. If they do interrupt, we are to expect that they do so respectfully and not rudely.

So, two action items that will help in this area are to, first, create the proper mindset, and second, set proper boundaries.

- **Create a proper mindset.** Develop the belief that your children aren't a bother and that you love interacting with them, no matter what. Think of the blessings they bring to your life. Reflect on the responsibility you have as caretakers of your children, who have been entrusted to you. Know you are preparing for future encounters when you're going to want them to let you know what's going on in their life.
- **Set proper boundaries.** You have stuff to do and things that need to get done. Be intentional about those tasks, and periods when you need to be off limits, and communicate when that is to your children. Some of those situations may be pre-established, so they recur at the same time every day or week. Be smart about when those times are so it makes the most sense for them and for you. For example, if you establish self-time for when they just arrive home from school, it won't serve either of you well.

The bottom line is that when you establish a welcoming response behavior, you're demonstrating a willingness to stop doing whatever you're doing and talk when you sense they are ready to engage . . . even if it's not the most opportune or ideal time. Believe me, the next crisis they encounter will never be a convenient time for you. Additionally, we want our children to feel like and know they are a blessing, and not a burden.

Reflection and Discussion Questions:

1. What's your typical initial reaction when your children request your assistance?

2. Is there an underlying mindset that is negatively affecting your response to your children? What do you think that is? Is it something you need to address?

Action Steps:

1. Practice being openly receptive when your kids interrupt or ask something of you, especially during time you'd normally react otherwise.

2. Create a small list of times or situations during the week when you'd prefer to be off-limits for interruptions, unless there is no other options for your kids. Share the list with them and discuss, as needed.

END WITH "OKAY?"

A subtle, yet highly effective word choice to help us reach agreement and buy-in from our children can be found in four simple letters. Those letters are "O.K.A.Y." (or "OK," if you prefer) followed by a question mark. Trust me . . . this is a keeper and it works. Here are some examples:

Without "Okay?"	With "Okay?"
Steven, it's time to set the table.	Steven, please set the table. Okay?
Mary, when you're done with your homework, put your books away.	Mary, when you're done with your homework, put your books away. Okay?
Ann, when this show is over, please turn the TV off.	Ann, when this show is over, please turn the TV off. Okay?
Mark, if the window is still spotty when you're done, you'll have to do it over.	Mark, if the window is still spotty when you're done, you'll have to do it over. Okay?
John, be sure to put gas in the car on your way home.	John, be sure to put gas in the car on your way home. Okay?

This strategy is simple but it's effective for a variety of reasons, including:

- It elicits a response. Because we've asked a question, it requires a response. Alternatively, simply making a statement doesn't really require a response.
- It creates buy-in. Because they've had to agree to something, they take more ownership of the decision, which increases compliance.
- It gives them a choice. Because of the way it's phrased, and follows on the heels of a request, it creates the impression that they have a choice in the decision instead of simply being told what to do.
- It minimizes a "No" response. As in the examples above, we're more likely to get a natural "Yes" response when we end with, "Okay?"
- They know that if they do what we're asking, it will please us.

By simply adding these two simple letters at the end of the sentence, the request is received as less threatening, often because your tone will come across as conversational versus confrontational.

Okay?

REFLECTION AND DISCUSSION QUESTIONS:

1. How much difficulty do you currently have getting your kids to respond when you ask something of them?
2. Describe how you'd like them to respond and what difference that would make.

ACTION STEPS:

1. Identify some common requests you now make of your children.
2. Practice (yes, practice) rephrasing your requests, so they end with "Okay?" like the examples above. Become aware and catch yourself when you don't use this method. With repetition it will become second nature.

Seek To Engage

Have you ever felt that getting your children to engage in a conversation can be a little like talking to a wall? I've been there. But if we step back and analyze why this is happening, we'll notice a pattern emerges. However, it's one that can be fixed—most of the time, anyway.

In-person, face-to-face conversations are still the most effective way to make a personal connection with another human being. However, in the technology age, which includes social media platforms, instant messaging, texting, and video conferencing, we have more ways than ever to avoid in-person dialogue.

What I've noticed with young people is that they now avoid even making a phone call if they can text or otherwise connect with their friends. As a result, they're losing their ability to have meaningful face-to-face conversations. That's why it's important that, from an early age through the teenage years, we consistently engage them in meaningful conversations so they learn the skill of effective communication.

Of course, conversation includes speaking and listening, which are skills that can be developed, if the desire is there to improve. As adults, often we're the ones who need to practice the art of communication. By modeling this skill with our children, they'll be better equipped to communicate with their friends, teachers, coaches, and eventual colleagues. In order to have meaningful conversation, both parties are to be involved: the person speaking and the person listening. With children especially, it's easier to initiate conversations in settings where they feel most comfortable and inclined to open up and talk. Driving in the car is often one of these places. However, with more and more kids (younger and younger) having their own phones and/or tablets, it's common for children to be engrossed in their handheld obsession while riding along, which can create a formidable barrier for communication.

Here's a tactical suggestion that may sound counterintuitive. But, hear me out. Since their devices can be a source of comfort and familiarity (I'm not saying that's good; it's just the way it is), allowing them to be on their device while we *initiate* a conversation allows them to keep their defenses down while we start to engage. However—and here's the trick—once the conversation takes on more meaning and significance, you'll often find that they naturally stop doing what they're doing and become engaged as well. Asking questions about non-threatening topics is one way to encourage this.

Granted, there will be times when the entertainment will be more captivating than our conversation. In those cases, we may need to request they refrain from using their phone while we talk. Or, if we're observant, we can notice when they naturally look up and take a break from eyeing their entertainment. At that moment, we have the perfect opportunity to initiate a discussion.

Alternatively, some families choose to implement a "no device policy" while in the car, period. If that is your rule, then stick with it and be consistent. Doing so may also help them establish the habit of not always being on their phone (especially in the car), so when your child is old enough to drive, it's not such an abrupt change in behavior.

The car can be an effective setting for having meaningful conversations for a couple of reasons:

- Our kids can't go anywhere. They can't walk away and don't usually choose to jump out of the moving car for fear of injury . . . and walking home isn't very appealing.
- It works because we're in a non-confrontational position. It's more conducive for engagement because we're not face-to-face, but instead seated alongside the child (if he's in the front seat). Standing and being face-to-face is usually a more confrontational posture.

Obviously, our approach and tone still matter. But we need to use caution with this strategy, as well. If each time we are in the car we start to interrogate our child and every drive turns into an inquisition, we'll have created an adversarial environment and will lose those opportunities. Other settings can also provide good opportunities for conversation, such as going for a walk, cooking together in the kitchen, playing catch, golfing, or washing the car. Try it. If we use these situations to produce noteworthy interactions, we'll find that, as our children grow older, these occasions may lead to some of our most meaningful memories.

REFLECTION AND DISCUSSION QUESTIONS:

1. What are some of the settings or opportunities you can identify that would be conducive for meaningful conversations?
2. What are some warning signs or clues that conversations with your child are headed in the wrong direction?

ACTION STEPS:

1. Look for settings for each of your children that are more comfortable for casual or in-depth conversations and seek to engage when those times occur.

2. Come up with a list of topics or lead-in discussions you can initiate that will be received positively to get conversations started.

INCLUDE YOUR KIDS

As our children grow and develop, it's good to remind ourselves that we're really commissioned with the responsibility of raising them to be adults. So, in addition to developing their character, shaping their values, and nurturing their talents, we are to also teach them how to function effectively as a contributing member of society.

For example, some parents are hesitant to include their kids in discussions about family finances and issues encountered at work. Are you? Perhaps you're cautious because you're not sure what's said in the kitchen will stay in the kitchen. Or you may believe they're not capable of understanding what you're talking about.

However, if we start including our children in these conversations at an early age (I recommend starting at around age nine) and they learn to keep personal information confidential, they're learning a life lesson that will serve them well as they form new relationships and eventually enter the workplace. In addition, as they hear the discussions we have around finances, balancing the budget, and saving for college or other events, they are learning what it takes to run a household, which will help them become more prepared for life on their own.

In addition to including our kids in practical household and life skill topics, we are inundated with a myriad of social and political worldviews that are impacting families like never before. As you know, those views are being spread 24-7 through cable news and social media channels, making it nearly impossible to isolate or protect our kids from being exposed or influenced by ideologies that may not align with our values and ideals.

If we're going to pass down our values and beliefs, we need to actively engage and share our views with our children from an early age. When they're young and even too innocent to fully understand, just allowing them to hear us discussing relevant issues prepares them to engage in those conversations with us as they age. Certainly it's not desirable for them to encounter alternate worldviews for the first time when they're talking with their friends or in class. Our kids knowing where we stand, and why we believe what we believe, forms a foundation they can firmly stand on when they are challenged or confronted as they mature.

Of course, some things you may choose not to disclose or share during the family talks. But, to completely avoid including them in meaningful conversations does not serve them well. Even if they resist and don't seem interested, they'll be absorbing more than you may recognize.

As always, let's be aware of our attitude and the language we use. Whether we're discussing work or finances or conflict with the neighbor, our kids will pick up on the attitude we display, as well as the approach we take toward solving problems. In these situations, do our kids witness our faith and trust in God, or do they primarily hear us worry, complain, or criticize? Ideally, we want to exhibit Christlike character and the fruit of the Spirit (Galatians 5:22-23), demonstrating how our faith intercepts and impacts our daily life decisions. One of our favorite family verses is, "Do everything without complaining and arguing, so that no one can criticize you" (Philippians 2:14).

Be reminded: it is desirable to positively discuss difficult times we're having at work—to let our kids observe how we navigate through challenges and come out stronger and better off. They'll face rough times when they start working as well. How do you want them to respond when difficulties arise? How they see us handle the mountains of life helps to prepare them for their own journey and the obstacles they will undoubtedly face along the way.

REFLECTION AND DISCUSSION QUESTIONS:

1. How often do you engage in conversations about work, finances, or life planning with the children present?
2. What are some things you could start including your kids in on a regular basis?

ACTION STEPS:

1. If this is a new practice, discuss the expectations including the discretion and confidentiality that will be required for them to participate in family discussions.
2. Involve them and ask their opinions and ideas or suggestions for how they think you could handle some of the issues that are discussed.

BE AUTHENTIC

My children need to see me be me. Your children need to see you be you. But, for them to see the real me, *I* need to know who I am first. And for your children to see the real *you*, you need to know who you are! Children are extremely perceptive. They can tell when we're being true to ourselves or faking it. If they see us carrying around a false identity, they're more likely to do the same.

One way we can test our own authenticity is to self-reflect: "Am I living with integrity, or not?" A life of integrity means that we're living an integrated life—a life truly reflective of the things we value and that give us energy. It means we're engaged in activities and work (volunteer or paid) we're passionate about. It means what we do when no one is watching is the same as we'd do if they were. It means we make decisions that are in our best interest, and not in conflict with what's truly important. When we do this, our kids will be more likely to learn and follow in our footsteps.

To help get some clarity around this concept, here's a simple three-step exercise to help you see how well you're aligned:

STEP ONE: IDENTIFY YOUR VALUES

What do you value most in life? I'd recommend doing a brain dump and just start writing down everything that comes to mind. Then, review your list. Narrow your list to the top five things you value most in life. Here are mine: faith, family, health, personal growth, and meaningful work.

Our values determine our priorities. Or, do they?

When you review your list, the values you listed should determine your priorities—the things that you do—the things that you take time for—the goals that you set—the things that make it onto your calendar.

STEP TWO: EXAMINE YOUR BEHAVIORS

As you review your values list, ask yourself this question, "Do my behaviors (what I do) support my values?" In almost every instance, when doing a values clarification exercise with people, health is identified as one of their top five values. So, if our health is something we value, for example, does our behavior reflect that we value our health? Are we eating well, getting adequate sleep, going to the doctor regularly, staying hydrated, and exercising?

Let's look at exercise, for example. If we say we value our health, then regular exercise is non-negotiable. If we don't exercise regularly or get enough regular daily activity, then we cannot truly say that we value our health. Why? You probably know there is nothing that we can do that will give us the health benefits that regular exercise gives!

You can plug any value into this example and it remains true. For example, if we said we value our family or our marriage, are we properly investing in those relationships in a manner that would demonstrate we really value them? We can't say we value our marriage if we don't spend quality time together, take time for each other, or seek to serve our spouse.

So, it's our actions that *identify* our true values. Or, we could say our actions reveal our true values. It's the things that we actually do: the things we spend time on, the things we spend money on, the goals that we set—even the things that we say. Those are the things that identify what our real values are. Whether we like it or not, our behavior is always communicating our values—always, always, always.

So, we bump up against this question: do our behaviors support our values? That's the million-dollar question, right?

Review, one more time, each of your values, and ask yourself, "Do my behaviors really support what I say I value?" And do you know what? Our kids are watching.

STEP THREE: CREATING ALIGNMENT

Maybe you've identified some things you say you value, but you really don't, based on how you're spending your time, money, and energy. So, make up a new list of the things you really do value. What is REALLY most important to you? Only then, when you've identified your true values, can you *assess whether your behaviors support and uphold your values*—those things that are most important to you.

Whatever values you have identified, what behaviors must align with and support those values? Wherever there are incongruences, what will it take for you to align your behaviors with what you value?

You'll find that when we align our behaviors with what it is we value, we are more likely to find the day-to-day motivation we need to stick to the changes we're seeking to make. Our values are the WHY that brings meaning and purpose to our life. If our kids are not part of that equation, obviously a change is in order.

Moving forward, we are well served to evaluate our list regularly. Each day presents its urgent challenges and temptations pulling us in one direction or another. But, when we evaluate our behavior over time, we can assess whether the choices we're making support those things we value. And if they don't, we can be proactive and seek out the help that will help us change. When we do, our children learn that life will pull and push us in different directions, trying to knock us off course. But, when we stay committed to our values and what's important, they learn firsthand how to successfully navigate through the storms of life.

As you work through this process, you'll discover if you're living a life aligned with who you are, what you value, and what gives you joy, purpose, and meaning. Our children need to know that we're authentic and living a life that reflects what's most important to us. It will help reassure them, and they'll relate better to who we are as they witness our lives in action.

REFLECTION AND DISCUSSION QUESTIONS:

1. If you're brave, have your spouse or a trusted friend (or your older children) describe what they know about you and what marks your life.

2. What brings you joy?

ACTION STEPS:

1. Identify a time this week, ideally, when you have ample uninterrupted time to complete the three-step exercise listed above.

2. What did you discover that you could act on immediately?

PRINCIPLE 42
AVOID TELLING

D o you like to be told what to do? If you do, you're the exception!
Regardless of age, whether young or old, no one likes to be told what to do. However, the phrase, "You need to . . ." can slip through our lips repeatedly in a day, especially when we're talking to our children. And to them, it may seem like they always "need" to do something—just ask them!

However, telling someone what to do unintentionally creates resistance in the person, even if they know it's the right or best thing to do. In his thought-provoking book, *Instant Influence,* Michael V. Pantalon, PhD, states, "If someone tells you to do something, you probably won't feel like doing it, even if you might otherwise have wanted to. In fact, the harder the other person tries to get you to do something—the more he yells at you, insists, threatens you with dire consequences—the less you're going to want to do it, and the less likely you are to actually do it."

For example, our pre-teen daughter had dressed and was waiting to go to a special event. When we saw that her pants had an obvious hole in an undesirable location, we told her, "You need to go change your pants!" Immediately, resistance ensued! Even though she knew she didn't want to go to the event wearing pants with a conspicuous hole, excuses about not having anything else to wear and not having time to change came instantly.

What happened in that brief exchange? Because of what was said, "You need to . . .," and how it was said, she was a bit embarrassed, and felt her judgment and ability to pick out clothes was being questioned. A better alternative would have been for us to start by asking her if she knew she had a hole in her pants. By doing so, she would have been given the benefit of the doubt and had an opportunity to proactively make the change. It would then have become more of her choice, which is what she wants.

Especially as our kids get older, our job isn't to tell them what to do as much as it is to present things that they may not have thought about before to help them in their decision. My college-age son was preparing for an important summer internship. In this situation, he sought out my input by asking for my opinion. Rather than telling him what I thought he should do, I gave him a couple of ideas he'd not previously considered . . . but I left the decision up to him.

Another good approach is to start your comments with, "If it were me, what I'd do is . . ." Of course, I know firsthand how well older kids (or adults) can respond to unsolicited advice! But whenever they open the door, I'm wanting to be aware and involved enough to recognize when my knowledge is desired.

We all like autonomy, even at an early age. And even though it seems counterintuitive, children are more likely to comply when they're not made to feel like they're being ordered to do something. So, rather than telling our young kids they need to do something, we're better off using an approach and choice of words that convey a similar message and still yields the desired result. For older children, function more like a peer and coach by putting yourself in their shoes and coming alongside to help guide and provide alternative choices, but allowing them to make and own the decision. The more you can accept this role, the more opportunities you'll have to be included in the decision making process as they face important life challenges.

Reflection and Discussion Questions:

1. How do you feel when someone tells you that you need to do something?
2. What are better word choices you can use when requesting something from your kids?

Action Steps:

1. Begin using the new word choices you came up with when you're making requests of your kids.
2. Give your kids permission to remind you if you revert to telling them what to do. It'll help increase your awareness and let them know it's a skill you're working to improve.

PRINCIPLE 43
OFFER CHOICES

A strategy that fits hand-in-glove with the previous principle is to provide our children with choices when asking them to do something. By providing a choice between two different options, we're setting them up for success and diffusing potential conflict. When given choices, they'll feel a sense of ownership for the outcome, instead of simply being told what to do . . . again!

Remember, no one likes to be told what to do. When we offer our children choices over what may be simply routine requests or tasks, they gain a sense of empowerment. And, having options helps them to learn to make decisions, versus simply complying with a request. Likewise, their response implies that an action will be taken.

In other words, "No" is not an option in the way the request is worded. Because they're led to make a declaration, it keeps the focus on what they're going to do, instead of what they're not going to do. That distinction increases their commitment to the choice they're about to make.

Here are some examples:

- "It's time to vacuum the house. Would you like to vacuum the upstairs or downstairs?"
- "It's time to clean the house. Would you like to vacuum or do the dusting?"
- "It's time to help make dinner. The gravy needs stirring, and the carrots need to be cut up. Which would you like to do?"
- "Will you be doing your homework before or after your practice today?"
- "You can either help your sister with her homework or help me with the laundry. Which one do you choose?"
- "You can either turn the television off now or not watch any TV tomorrow. What's your choice?"
- "Are you going to exercise before or after you practice piano?"

The authoritarian parent will probably scoff at this suggestion. The authoritarian parent is all about command and control. You know, "Do what I say, when I say, because I say it!" While that may produce the short-term result you're looking for, it'll come at the expense of your relationship with your children. And, it will do nothing to help your children make decisions and learn that every decision has a consequence, either good or bad.

Over Christmas, my brother-in-law and his wife were at the hotel pool with their three boys and daughter, who is the youngest. She was getting tired, so her parents decided it was time for her to be done and to take her back to the room to change. At the time, she'd been standing at the edge of the pool and jumping into her dad's arms, much to her delight.

So, her dad asked her a question that made all the difference. He said, "It's time to go—

how many jumps should we do, three or four?"

To which his four-year-old daughter said, "Four, Daddy." Brilliant!! It worked so well because, instead of stopping the activity without her input, they gave her a choice after stating it was time to go. She had say-so in the decision. They also informed her of what was coming—it was time for her to be done. When the four jumps were over, there was no objection . . . no complaining.

Of course, the choices and options we present to our children will depend on their age and appropriateness of the situation. Generally, providing only two choices is also the better option, versus three or more choices, especially for younger children.

If our kids are always being forced to do things, it can become a very negative environment and not fun to be around. Is that the kind of environment we want to create and foster in our homes?

Reflection and Discussion Questions:

1. How do you describe your current parenting style? How would your children describe it?

2. How would you describe the parenting approach your parents had with you? Do you see yourself repeating it, either positively or negatively? How?

Action Steps:

1. Think of some common duties or chores you ask your children to do. Modify your requests so that it includes a choice.

2. Identify what's working and what isn't and alter your communication, so you get a better response.

ASK THEM TO CHOOSE

No matter their age, most of the time, children relish having the undivided attention of their parents. Even more so, they love setting the agenda. In today's busy world, with a to-do list that only seems to expand and never get completed, it's very common for parents to forget that spending time with their children is one of the most valuable investments they can make. Remember, kids spell love: T-I-M-E.

To help assure the investment is worthwhile and yields a meaningful return, here's a twist to an idea that will yield big dividends. Start by picking a time that works (a time that you MAKE work) for both your child and you, without it being pre-arranged. Then, approach him or her and ask what he or she would like to do for the next ___ minutes. (For younger kids, you won't even have to put a time qualifier on it because they may not have the attention span to do it for very long. For older kids, it can be helpful to set the parameter because it creates a reasonable expectation. But it's up to you, depending on the situation, to be up front with how much time you have available to spend with them.)

When they respond, just say, "Okay," no matter what—unless it is something totally unreasonable, like jumping out the window or coloring the walls with permanent marker. For younger kids, it might be playing with Legos or trucks or coloring or riding bikes, or something like that. The point is—it's their choice. They get to pick the activity and you're an exciting, willing participant.

For older kids, it might be playing a video game or shooting hoops or cooking or (if you're lucky) just talking. Again, it doesn't matter what it is. They get to choose what it is you're going to do together.

A similar approach is to invite them into an activity you're doing or getting ready to do. This is especially impactful if it's something in which you already know they have an interest. For example, when something needs to get fixed around the house, it's almost always easier and less time consuming to just do it myself. I remember when our daughter was young, she enjoyed *helping* me fix things. So, if I had a project in the garage or a sink that wasn't working, I would at times ask if she'd like to help, much to her delight. These situations not only create a shared experience, but they also allow for teaching and learning of skills our kids wouldn't be exposed to otherwise.

During this time, do your very best to impose a no-cell-phone or no-interruption policy for both of you. This is your one-on-one time, which unfortunately in most families is a rare occurrence. When the time is up, be sure to convey that you enjoyed the time together and mention something specific about your interaction to reaffirm your comments. If you've not done this with your kids, or don't do it very often, be ready for their shock-and-surprise reaction . . . it'll be priceless!

REFLECTION AND DISCUSSION QUESTIONS:

1. When is the last time you approached your child and gave him or her 30 minutes of undivided attention, and made it his or her choice for what you'll do?

2. How can you create the bandwidth to allow more time with each child?

ACTION STEPS:

1. Look at your schedule and identify when you can create opportunities to make time for these meaningful exchanges with your kids.

2. Insist on no interruptions, unless it's an emergency, once the activity begins.

PRINCIPLE 45
HELP YOUR KIDS SET GOALS

As a parent, watching our children accomplish feats we never even imagined provides us with enormous joy and fulfillment. I believe all kids have within them an innate desire to do great things. It's how they're wired. When I was a kid, driving the tractor up and down the field, I'd look up at the vast sky, enamored with the jets flying to and fro high above. I imagined that someday that would be me, even though I'd never even set foot on a plane. Now, in my job and as an author and speaker, that is me.

One of the privileges we have with our children is to help facilitate the desires of their hearts. What we have to safeguard against is doing anything that would deflate, dissuade, or discourage what is an inborn desire or passion. We also have to be cautious to not project our desires onto them, if it would be counter to who God made them to be—especially if it's primarily for our satisfaction and so we can feel good about what they do, whether that's to fulfill our unmet accomplishments or to impress our family and friends. Generally it'll take kids getting into their teenage years before they'll start fleshing out what they're gifted at and discover the desires that are starting to well up inside them. Up until that point, we want to pick up clues by simply observing the tendencies they have, what they like to spend time doing, whom they like to be with, and what they talk about. Once we have a sense, our job is to nourish and help them define more clearly what their goals are.

Keep in mind, it's not always easy to decipher what goals they have, but there will be clues—some obvious, but others not so much. When we moved to Colorado, our oldest daughter was starting her junior year in high school and switched from being a soccer player to a runner. She had good success that year, both in cross country and track. During the summer before her senior year, one day I noticed there was a poster in her room that she'd made, listing her goals for her final year in high school.

I was impressed. Not only were her goals loftier than I'd have had for her, but they were also very specific (which is an essential element for goal setting). Since she'd laid out her goals, I wanted to figure out how I could come alongside her to help make them a reality. What is common, and what she'd done, is to establish outcome goals. In other words, her goals stated what she wanted to have happen or accomplish in three areas: cross country, school, and track. She'd successfully answered the first question in setting goals: What do I want? In addition, she'd written them out and posted them in her room so she'd see them every day— they were tangible.

It became clear that she'd not clearly answered the second question: What price am I willing to pay? Shortly after I'd seen her goals, we sat together on the front porch and discussed her goals. In a brief period of time, with her pen and paper, I walked her through each of her goals and had her write out what she'd need to do—what price she was willing to pay—to reach her goals. I encouraged her to focus on this part . . . the process. While she established what outcome she wanted, she couldn't control the outcome, only the process of paying the price she was willing to pay.

During this discussion, the best way for me to help her was to use the coach approach. At no time did I inject what I thought she needed to do. I simply asked the right questions to draw out from her what she already knew. These were her goals. Since she was the initiator and creator of the goals, and now having identified the price she'd be willing to pay, it more fully insured that she had total ownership of the goals. With that foundation, you can probably see how she can use her process goals to hold herself accountable, and allow me or anyone else to be her accountability partner, as well.

So, now she'd established the what and how of achieving her goals. The final step was to answer the question: Why are these important for you? While she thought she knew, it was good for her to contemplate a bit more deeply why these goals were important and clarify their significance. (You'll find an alternative goal and accountability system in Appendix 2).

How did it work? Well, she accomplished seven of her nine goals, including three state championships. What was my role? Only to be aware of the path she was on and provide guidance by asking the right questions so she had a plan to follow on the way to her goals.

Has it always worked out that way? No. But what a joy it is as parents when we can follow their development progress and, when the time is right, be in a position to facilitate, coax, encourage, and support what is blossoming inside of them. Don't let the thought and possibility of failure prevent you from engaging in this process. Remember, there's no such thing as failure, only feedback. Simply start by answering the three questions and adjust as needed along the way.

Let your kids surprise you! Be that source of support and help them accomplish what they can't do on their own. By teaching them this goal-setting formula, you're giving them a gift they'll be able to use in every area of life, for the rest of their life.

REFLECTION AND DISCUSSION QUESTIONS:

1. Are you able to identify some of the passions and desires that your kids have developed? What are they?

2. How familiar are you with the goal-setting process? Do you currently set goals regularly? Why or why not?

ACTION STEPS:

1. Identify a time when you can sit with your child and initiate the goal-setting process described above.

2. Follow the same process for yourself, if you haven't already done so.

Be a Promise Keeper

Have you ever wanted to confuse your kids and set them up for failure and you for frustration? Probably not, right? But, if we're not mindful of keeping our promises, unfortunately, that is exactly the scenario we could unintentionally create.

To ensure this doesn't happen, we should follow this fundamental principle: do what we say we're going to do. If for some reason we can't, then we want to immediately acknowledge it and apologize. In other words, when we make a promise, we're compelled to keep it. In order to implement this principle, it's critically important to stop and think if we really mean what we're about to say.

Our goal is to establish trust. Kids absorb what we say. They evaluate whether we're true to our word and if they can trust what we say and do. And, since they're likely to repeat what they see us doing, we're establishing a framework for their life, as well. Do you want your kids to be trustworthy? If so, it's essential we're worthy of trust.

It doesn't matter how big or little the promise is; the same principle applies. When we tell our kids we're going to do something, it may not seem like a huge deal to us, but it is to them.

This scenario is in play any time we make a request or respond to a request of our kids. For example, your young daughter comes to you while you're reading and asks you to play with her. In response, you say something to the effect of, "Sure, just give me five minutes." What happens when 15 minutes later, you're still reading? You've broken a promise and lost trust.

Or, your teenage son is playing video games. You let him know he has five minutes to finish, to which he says, "Okay." What happens when, 10 minutes later, you see he's still playing and ignore it? He's learned that what you say doesn't matter, and he doesn't need to honor you or your requests.

Or, your 16-year-old daughter agrees to pick up her room before going to a movie with her friends. What do you do when they come to pick her up, but she hasn't touched her room? If she's allowed to go, so they won't be late, she's learned you don't really mean what you say.

Of course, the natural consequence is for her to pick up her room properly before leaving. If she's late, she's late. She'll most likely be upset with you, but you'll want to be prepared for that and not let her see it affect your mood. You had an agreement, and she didn't comply, so there's a natural, appropriate consequence.

If scenarios like these are a rare occurrence, the negative impact may be negligible. But, if we stick to our word sometimes, but other times don't follow through, we're creating confusion and undermining trust. Our unpredictability suggests that trust is a variable, instead of an honored principle of healthy living.

So, the takeaway is this: no matter what we say, we have to make sure to follow through and do what we say. For times when we unfortunately fail, we simply and clearly acknowledge we didn't keep our word and sincerely apologize. Doing so conveys we value our word and that trust is a quality we aspire to both exemplify and instill.

REFLECTION AND DISCUSSION QUESTIONS:

1. Are you consistent in following through when making a request of your child? Rate yourself on a scale from 1 to 10.

2. How diligent are you about keeping promises—even little ones—when you tell your kids you're going to do something? Rate yourself on a scale from 1 to 10. If you're not sure, ask your kids.

ACTION STEPS:

1. Stop or pause and think before making a request to make sure you can do what you say you're going to do.

2. Practice your apologies and apologize when you fail to follow through.

PRINCIPLE 47

Become Better at Life

Do you have regular family meeting times? "For what?" you might ask. Regular weekly meetings serve multiple purposes, including using the time for a family devotional, reviewing the upcoming week of activities, sharing any victories family members had the previous week, as well as any unique challenges that may have occurred. (If some kids are out of the house already, perhaps they can attend using video technology like Zoom or Facetime.)

As parents, our role is helping our children grow in all dimensions of life throughout their time with us. We want to positively influence them, so they're equipped when they go out on their own. One of the primary responsibilities we bear is shaping their character while they're under our roof. To facilitate this process, ask this question, "What personal qualities do we hope they attain, and who is God calling them to be?"

The "Better at Life" exercise is one we can add to family meeting times. If you're not yet having family meeting times, I suggest you begin by doing it around the dinner table after a meal, for example. The exercise is designed to facilitate a dialogue, solicit feedback, and receive accountability from those who know us best and care for us the most.

The purpose of the exercise is to help our children become better at life by reducing bad habits and behaviors, which affect their character development and personal growth. The process will also nudge us into becoming better parents. It probably obvious that people who know us best are also most equipped to point out our blind spots.

If you're not sure when to do it, just pick a time and get the process started. Here's how the process works:

- All family members write down one thing they personally did well that week. They then write down one thing/behavior they did that week that could use improvement.
- Next, in turn, everyone states out loud one thing they feel that each of the other family members did well during the last week. The family member receiving the feedback writes down all the comments that have been given.
- Then, everyone states one thing they feel the other family members could do better. The person receiving the feedback can only respond by saying, "Thank you." No other comments can be made affirmatively or argumentatively.
- Lastly, all family members review the suggestions they received, along with the one area of self-identified improvement. From that list, they pick one or two things to improve. That becomes their focus for the next week.

Keep in mind the primary emphasis of the "Better at Life" exercise is on character qualities, as opposed to being a better cook, for example. Being a great chef is a good quality to have, but this exercise intentionally focuses on character. Too often character development is ignored in favor of performance-related outcomes. God cares much more about our character than our accomplishments, which is why we strive to purposely nurture character development.

The first few times your family engages in this exercise, it'll be normal for the feedback and suggestions to seem a bit superficial. However, after a few weeks, provided the feedback is honest and sincere, trust will deepen, as will the information that is shared. Soon, this exercise will become one of the highlights of the week and prove to be one of the most valuable tools in your arsenal.

Reflection and Discussion Questions:

1. What times each week are most conducive for all your family members to meet?
2. What conflicts can you anticipate that you'll need to overcome?

Action Steps:

1. Determine what you all want to focus on during your meeting time. Create a general outline and share what is decided.
2. Start. Don't worry about perfection! Just dive in and set whatever ground rules will help achieve the desired outcome.

PRINCIPLE 48.1
BE A ROLE MODEL – PART 1

Monkey see, monkey do. Ever heard that expression? Guess what! It applies to little monkeys even more than big ones. Kids are sponges! They acutely, and subconsciously, absorb what they see us doing. How we're behaving impacts them much more than what they hear us saying.

So, ask yourself, *What are my kids observing and absorbing?*

In this section, we'll briefly explore three value-related decisions, followed by three additional areas in the next section. As you review these life choices, consider if there are adjustments you could make, so your monkeys are acquiring the behaviors you'd like them to copy.

1. Time

The most valuable resource we possess is time. We'll spend all the time we have. How we *invest* it will determine our future. It is the one resource that isn't renewable and one we can never get back. Once a minute is spent, it's gone forever.

In my work as a life coach, I've often heard the comment, "I don't have enough time." In reality, everyone (including you) has 1,440 minutes in a day or 168 hours in a week. No one has more time than anyone else. How we invest the minutes and hours we have available leaves an impression from which our kids will learn. For example, if we constantly belabor how busy we are, they'll draw conclusions about what they can ask of us in the moment, and what they can expect in life.

How we use our time influences how our kids will spend their time, especially after they're out of our house and on their own. By managing our priorities effectively, we're giving them proper training for that next stage in life.

What's most important to us will evolve as we go through different life stages. In order to live according to our priorities, we of course need to know what they are and ensure they are aligned very closely with our values.

Since we have kids, obviously they're a priority. If we're alive, our health is a priority. If we want to survive and provide opportunities for our family, generating income is a priority. If we're married, the relationship with our spouse is a priority. Assuming you're a Christ-follower, your relationship with Christ is a priority. What other priorities do you have in your life?

To reiterate, as we assess and live our life, we want to be aware that how our kids see us managing our activities will impact how they learn to manage theirs. In addition, if our behavior is incongruent with what we tell them is important, they're learning that what we say doesn't really matter.

The main tip that will help is this: schedule your priorities—literally put them in your calendar. I've learned from coaching others, as well as from personal experience, the adage, "What gets scheduled gets done," is astute advice.

As much as possible, schedule in your calendar for the week every essential must-do item (work schedule, sleep, etc.). Then fill out the remainder of calendar with your highest priority activities, which mimic what it is you say you value.

If you try this for a few weeks, you'll be amazed at how it changes your productivity, your relationships, and your life. Will your ideal schedule always happen? No, but by having a plan, it's much more likely to be realized.

2. Faith

It's our responsibility as Christian parents to help our kids grow in character and in their faith and relationship with Christ. The way we impact their growth in these areas is for them to see us growing in our faith and character. We want to prepare the heart and mind of our kids to know Jesus. We can't do that unless we do. They will know that by how we go through life with them, from the earliest stages.

It'll be the things they see us doing to grow in our faith that will leave an imprint. In addition to telling them to read their Bible, think of how impactful it is to see us reading ours and regularly engaging in daily quiet time to meditate, pray, and read Scripture. Personally, my preferred quiet time for reading Scripture, meditating, and praying is early morning, usually before the kids are up. But when they do get up early, or if I get up late, they'll know where to find me.

Do they participate with us as we go to church every week, or only on special holidays, or just when we feel like it? Do they witness us praying regularly for them and for others?

Do they see us consistently financially supporting our church, regardless of personal financial peaks and valleys? Are they aware of the financial support we're giving to other Christ-centered or non-profit organizations?

Do they see us serving to meet the needs of the poor? Do they see us spending time practicing good deeds and helping out those who are struggling with life?

Do they see us living out our faith in the real world? What they see us doing, rather than what they hear you preaching, is how we'll best help them feel secure and grow in their faith.

One practice I started doing at the end of my quiet time in the morning is to share a Bible verse. I'll pick one verse from the Bible chapter I read in the morning and share it on our family group text. Not every day, but often it's given a thumbs-up or heart.

Just to clarify, none of this is done as a prerequisite for securing our salvation; Christ already did that. But the Christian life does require a change in behavior, including practicing disciplines to help us grow in faith.

Frequently, I meet with parents and hear stories of how their kids have "left the faith." Our role is to lay a proper foundation, instilling the values we hold, and setting an example that they want to emulate. There are no guarantees. As our children leave home, they'll be influenced in many different directions. What they experience while under our care will also greatly influence the choices they end up making. By modeling faith at home, you'll know you've done what you can to set them on the right path.

3. Health

As parents, it's also our responsibility to help our children develop and grow physically, which includes adopting healthy habits. In addition, it's imperative for them to learn that their choices are important and come with consequences.

The most effective way we can communicate this message is by making good choices ourselves. Health is a broad topic, but there are a few essential behaviors that we can model for our kids, which will ultimately influence them.

We have to be cautious, however, because it's easy to want them to be our clones and do what we do. But remember, and be assured, some of the behaviors they see you model won't become evident in their lives until they're adults and fully making decisions for themselves. Here are some health-related habits to strive for:

- Exercise
- Sleep
- Nutrition
- Hydration
- Moderation

The best way for our kids to catch on to what is important to us is by observation of our example—more so than just by hearing what we say. Francis of Assisi said, "It is no use walking anywhere to preach unless our walking is our preaching." The same is true of the words we use with our kids. When they see what we do and it aligns with our instruction, they are fortified in their resolve to do the same.

REFLECTION AND DISCUSSION QUESTIONS:

1. Of the three areas listed, which one do you feel you are excelling at and closely modeling what you'd aspire for your kids to do, as well? Why is that?

2. Of the three areas, which one do you feel you could improve the most? Why is that, and what's holding you back?

ACTION STEPS:

1. From each of the three areas, pick one change—one improvement—you're willing to make that would have a significant impact on what you'd like to model for your children and would be good for you, as well.

2. Share with your children the change you're making and why you feel it's important.

Be a Role Model – Part 2

ow that you've reviewed and started to take action on the previous three value-related decisions, here are three more common areas we can assess and look to improve. The guidelines and ideas presented are to give you food for thought. What you ultimately decide will be based on what you feel is important and will make a difference in the lives of both you and your kids. There isn't a formula or *right* answer. Every choice should reflect what it is you value most and would speak the loudest to your children.

So, with that framework, let's consider three more areas:

1. Finances

Money talk can either dominate a family's conversation or be non-existent. There doesn't seem to be much gray area for financial talk. It's either a part of the family dialogue or not at all.

But how will our kids learn how to effectively manage their future financial resources if they don't learn at home? I think you'll agree that economics taught in the classroom is largely theory. It doesn't prepare or teach our kids the real-life experiences best learned by understanding how we manage our household expenses (provided we're setting a good example).

Many helpful resources are available to teach and train financial strategies like getting out of debt, budgeting, and investing. Seek those out if you need help in this area.

However, here are a few principles for you to consider that will help your kids establish a healthy relationship with money:

- Involve all family members in the financial process, so everyone can observe and learn firsthand. Allow your children to understand how you earn your income and what you did to achieve the level of success that you've achieved. It's important they understand your background and the work and sacrifices you've made to reach your current level of income, no matter what it is.

- Openly practice gratitude. Any time money comes into your home, develop the habit of giving thanks. Let your kids see you being thankful and grateful for what you have been given, versus being stressed out over finances.

- Make the commitment to give a percent or flat amount back to your church. Figure out what amount you are willing to start with and build up from there. God will bless your commitment.

- Develop your financial plan so you can give about ten percent toward your savings account. If you have debt, work to systematically pay it off. If needed, get help developing a plan with a target date and start small. Involve your family with any sacrifices you're willing to make to achieve your debt-free goal.

- Establish a monthly budget and live within the parameters you set, no matter what. It's a good practice to track every expense, so the family members can see where the money is going.

- Become smart financially. Depending upon your situation, work to create alternative sources of sustainable income, in addition to whatever salary may be coming in. Encourage your kids to contribute and, as is age appropriate, foster their entrepreneurial mindset. Help them learn business principles by practicing them.

- Establish and stick to the wonderfully hard concept of delayed gratification by thinking long term. Start saving up for special purchases or vacations. This strategy will allow everyone to experience the joy of seeing a goal attained, without it being a stress-filled experience.

- Pray daily for God's provision: pray He opens doors, and that what you do is aligned with your skills, talents, and abilities . . . and with His will.

The best way to prepare and equip your kids to effectively manage finances is for them to become involved firsthand by learning what it takes to run your household. It will require extra effort on your part, but the payback for them and you will be worthwhile.

2. Relationships

The most important relationship your kids will witness is the relationship between you and your spouse. Ideally, the family unit is intact and both parents are in the home. Even if the parents are split, the way the parents communicate with each other, and the quality of the relationship they maintain, will impact the hearts of our kids.

Fathers, is it obvious to your children by what they see you doing and the attitude you demonstrate toward your wife that you are lovingly serving her? For wives, is it apparent to your kids that respect emanates from you toward your husband in how you treat, talk to, and support him?

If the husband maintains a spirit of love, kindness, and devotion, and the wife conveys an attitude of respect and joyfulness, then the words your kids hear will be consistent with what they see each of you doing.

As a result, they are more likely to demonstrate an attitude of love and respect toward each other, toward you, and with their eventual spouse.

Before kids, couples have together time whenever they want—it's just the two of them. Date nights are easier to plan and spontaneous outings can spring up whenever the urge hits. But after kids, this all changes. If the parents are willing to leave their new addition with someone else, even for a couple hours, babysitters have to be arranged, and of course the bedtime routine could be interrupted. Then there's the sicknesses and everything else that wasn't a consideration prior to being parents.

It's common for new parents to pour themselves 100 percent into their baby and neglect to take time away for themselves. The demands on their time and energy only increase when more kids are added to the household. As much as their children need nourishment and care, so does the couples' relationship. Therefore, it's best for parents to establish the mindset and routine of making regular alone time part of their parenting repertoire after the birth of their first child.

With intentional planning, here's a solid recommendation you can follow, which will help you stay connected and grow closer even after kids come along.

- One weekly date night—just the two of you for dinner and a movie, or something like that. Be creative. Your dates don't have to be lengthy or expensive, so do what your time and financial budget will allow. But, be willing to sacrifice for yourself as well as for your kids. Maybe your date is a picnic dinner and walk in the park, or a round of golf, or bowling, or dancing. The idea is to get away and focus on you and enjoy being together. Keep talk about your kids to a minimum and refocus on each other.

- Once a quarter have a weekend getaway. Again, with proper planning, you can make your mini-retreat as extravagant or as simple as you'd prefer. These quarterly outings will do wonders to rejuvenate you physically, emotionally, and relationally. You could take one of these weekends to attend a marriage enrichment retreat led by trained facilitators. Think out of the box and create a weekend you'll forever remember.

- Once a year, take a week vacation—just the two of you—away from the kids. If you're not already in the habit of doing this, you may think this is crazy. But, if you want to give your best to your kids, taking time away and remembering why you fell in love and started a family will pay dividends in deepening your relationship. Enlist family or friends to help make this possible. Maybe exchange the favor with another couple, so they can enjoy a week away, as well.

In addition to enhancing your relationship, these planned times together do wonders for sending a message to your kids that they aren't always your number one priority—your spouse is. To incorporate these weekly, quarterly, and annual touch points with each other, you'll most likely miss some of your kids' activities. Be okay with that. As they get older, they will appreciate the effort you put into nourishing your marriage amid the array of activities and events that often take precedent each week. Keep in mind, they're more likely to emulate what they see you do as a married couple after they get married and start a family, especially when they see the pay off!

Of all the things you can do for your children, keeping your marriage intact and thriving will put them ahead in every key indicator there is for children to be successful in life. If you've neglected this area, it's not too late. Simply start the planning and take action today!

3. Entertainment

The choices we make for entertainment, including what we listen to, watch, and do, convey what's important to our kids. We want our selections to be congruent with what it is we say we value. Then, what we encourage, and the forms of entertainment we allow for our kids, should also be aligned with those values.

But, it starts with us. Our kids are looking to see if what we say is consistent with what we do. For example, do you restrict what they watch, but have your own video collection including games or movies that are inappropriate, based on your declared value system?

When watching something as a family and something inappropriate comes across the screen, how do you react? Do you ignore what you're viewing and allow it to continue? Or, depending on the content, use the content as an opportunity to discuss why it's inappropriate, so they gain a sense of confidence when making their own entertainment decisions?

Entertainment has some value and can be included into a weekly routine. But with the Internet and social media so readily available, even busy, responsible adults get sucked into spending too much time surfing the net or engaged in social media sites.

As stated earlier, it's safe to say that the advancements in technology have easily outpaced our ability to manage it. What viewing habits have you adopted that your kids are observing in you? We can't expect children to manage their time if we're not effectively managing how we spend our entertainment time and the choices we make.

Just like it's reasonable to limit the total amount of screen time for your kids, set parameters for yourself. Depending on your situation, what's a reasonable amount of total screen time (for entertainment purposes) to establish for them? How about for you?

Screen time includes any device with a display including smartphone, TV, tablet, computer, etc. Entertainment includes watching/reading the news, surfing the net, video games, social media, movies, shows, etc. It's currently estimated that the average elementary-age student engages in six hours of screen time per day!

It's easier to allow unrestricted use of devices and unfiltered entertainment choices. But we're not called to be parents who take the easy way out. We are called to step into the battlefield as many times as necessary to guide our kids safely through the minefield of entertainment.

If we allow their minds to be filled with unhealthy, unwholesome, and unproductive entertainment, we are failing in our responsibility. If we do it ourselves, we're also neglecting to set the example, establish credibility, and model the behavior they need to see in us.

Regarding location, it's highly recommended to never allow kids to have either a TV or a computer in their room and that whatever they're watching be observable. Regarding filters, always make sure security and permission filters are set up and properly monitored, when possible. Not only does it prevent our kids from being tempted, but it also prevents us from unneeded temptation as well.

REFLECTION anD DISCUSSION QUESTIONS:

1. Of the three areas listed, which one do you feel you are excelling at and closely modeling what you'd aspire for your kids to do, as well? Why is that?
2. Of the three areas, which one do you feel you could improve the most? Why is that and what's holding you back?

ACTION STEPS:

1. From each of the three areas, pick one change—one improvement—you're willing to make that would have a significant impact on what you'd like to model for your children and would be good for you, as well.
2. Share with your children the change you're making a change and why you feel it's important.

MAKE TIME FOR DINNER

Without a doubt, in the later years of my life, the fondest memories will include reminiscing about dinnertime conversations we had with our children. For the most part, mealtimes have been when we've laughed the hardest, shared the most, and left feeling more connected with each other.

Unfortunately, in today's family dynamic, with endless activities for both parents and kids, the ritual of family dinnertime seems almost like a relic of times gone by. Well, I believe it's time to resurrect this very important family tradition!

Not convinced yet? Anne Fishel, Ph.D., at TheFamilyDinnerProject. org, states, "Over the past 15 years, researchers have confirmed what parents have known for a long time: sharing a family meal is good for the spirit, the brain, and the health of all family members. Recent studies link regular family dinners with many behaviors that parents pray for: lower rates of substance abuse, teen pregnancy, and depression, as well as higher grade-point averages and self-esteem."

According to the American Academy of Pediatrics, studies also indicate that dinner conversation is a more potent vocabulary booster than reading, and the stories told around the kitchen table help our children build resilience. The icing on the cake is that regular family meals also lower the rates of obesity and eating disorders in children and adolescents.

Here are some tips for protecting the sacred meal:

- Refrain from having the television on and make sure all hand-held devices are more than an arm's reach away from the table (and preferably out of sight).
- Be flexible and adjust the mealtime daily, if needed, to accommodate varying schedules and activities that will undoubtedly interfere.
- Have the kids who are available help prepare the meal; acknowledge their contribution during the meal.
- Let everyone know ahead of time approximately when mealtime will be that night, so they can plan and allow time for eating together.
- Develop a standard so only one conversation occurs at a time, and practice not interrupting anyone else. Allowing each child the opportunity to share is invaluable, even if they don't always have much to contribute.
- As the parents, have some fun facts or interesting observation to generate conversation. For kids who are hesitant to participate in the discussion, bringing up a topic of interest to them will more likely increase their engagement.

Believe that putting forth the extra effort to allow for family mealtimes is a worthy investment. It's the memories that will be cherished forever, but there are a lot more benefits as well!

REFLECTION AND DISCUSSION QUESTIONS:

1. Take inventory. How many times per week now does your family eat together for dinner?
2. What changes will you have to make so you're able to have more meals together each week?

ACTION STEPS:

1. Pick a time and let your family know about having more dinners together, so all are aware and can make changes need to make it happen.
2. Prepare for your meals by having some conversation starters, if needed, especially ones that will include all family members.

Take Time to Celebrate

In our performance-driven culture, focusing on the next thing to do, along with achieving the next big goal, has become an obsession. There's always more to do and, seemingly, never enough time to get it done. Our kids are encouraged to get good grades, ace the test, be at the top of the class, and win the race. But there is always more homework to do, tests to take, and events to perform.

So, when do we take time to celebrate the small or large achievements that are being accomplished? Unfortunately, it's often only after the big and notable victories, if at all, along with other major events like birthdays.

As an embarrassing confession, I regrettably remember many occasions that were cause for celebration, but I didn't take advantage of the opportunity. They included everything from good grades to awards, and from performances to scholarships. I wish those opportunities could be put on rewind for a do-over. But they can't. In fact, I was searching my memory hoping to provide you with a positive example of a time when we did plan and intentionally celebrate their successes. But nothing came to mind.

Our college kids all earned significant athletic and academic scholarships to their chosen institution. Did we celebrate that? No. Our daughter was a multiple-event state champion in track and cross-country. Did we celebrate? No. No real celebrations for any of their achievements. Of course, we took pictures and gave high-fives and hugs, and did the obligatory birthday celebrations, but that was about it. I do regret that.

And remember, we don't just have to only celebrate their wins. We can also take time to celebrate the effort they put into whatever they are working toward, whether they win or not. Celebrating their effort and the work they put into something reinforces that we value effort, not just great outcomes.

However, if you're like me and can't have a do-over, the celebrations that have been missed can be acknowledged by having one BIG party to make up for those missed—and then we can do differently, from then on. This event will be to recognize occasions you remember you could have celebrated but didn't. Then, moving forward, make it a point to have small celebrations along the way, and major celebrations for momentous events.

As a side note, our brains are purposefully rewired to notice more of the positive things when we take even a brief moment to acknowledge and recognize those that do happen. As a result, our focus shifts to start noticing more positive things that occur throughout the day, which impacts how we feel and perform. That's a pretty good gift to give our kids.

REFLECTION AND DISCUSSION QUESTIONS:

1. How well do you currently celebrate even small achievements or accomplishments?
2. Is there something coming up you could celebrate that would be unexpected and appreciated?

ACTION STEPS:

1. At the beginning of each month, look ahead so you can plan and prepare for events that would be worthy of celebration.
2. Have party supplies on hand at all times so when unexpected successes happen you're able to quickly put together a celebration.

TEACH MANNERS

As a parent, what grabs your attention when your kids' friends come over? If you're like me, it's the kids who practice good manners. Even though they are rarely observed, proper manners are noticeable because they make us feel respected and appreciated.

One thing I so admire about all our kids are the friends they've chosen. In addition to having shared values, their friends demonstrate respect and manners when they are around us. An advantage of your kids bringing their friends into your home is that you get to see them up close and personal. We can tell a lot about them and their families by how they talk, what they say, and how they interact with us. It's always a joy to hear them genuinely say, "Thank you," when we give them a ride or have them over for a meal.

Manners are best taught by modeling them to others, including to our kids. Perhaps you've noticed a recurring theme in this book: anything we expect or require of our kids is best taught by who we are and what we do . . . our being and our doing.

Here are a few basic manners to instill in your children that will serve them well:

- Say, "Please," and, "Thank you," often. Almost every request should be accompanied with "Please" and anything that's received should be acknowledged with "Thank you." This may sound elementary, but how often have you received a compliment and brushed it off or discounted it, instead of simply accepting it and saying, "Thank you," in response?
- Listen to the other person who is talking and ask a follow-up question about what was said.
- Avoid talking about yourself, and be genuinely interested in the other person. Focus on being interested, instead of being interesting.
- Don't interrupt another person (this includes kids, too, even if it is a sibling). Patiently wait for an opportunity to speak, as you listen with a desire to understand. An exercise that can help teach this habit is to have an object that can be passed around the table, like a towel or plastic cup or stuffed animal, and the only person who can speak is the person who has the item placed by their plate.
- Never be the first person to put food on your plate. Always offer the dish or food item to someone else first.
- Have everyone wait for the food to be served before the eating begins, unless the okay has been given to start. If it's a large group, wait until the person to your right and left have been served their meals before eating.
- Ask to be excused from the table and make sure your chair is pushed in before walking away.
- Ask if any help is needed while the meal is being prepared.
- If you can, provide help to clean up after the meal, or just pitch in when it is time to wash dishes.
- Identify a compliment you can make about the meal and say it out loud.

- During the first encounter with people, genuinely identify something about them or what they're wearing to compliment.
- Send handwritten thank-you notes for any gift received or courtesy extended to you, or just because.

And, our kids learn from their friends as well. I recall when our daughter went over to her friend Loren's house for the afternoon and evening. When I picked her up that night, she said, "Loren is about the nicest person I know. She is so kind and has the best manners." That example exemplifies why the friends they chose are one of the most important choices they'll make growing up.

The habits kids adopt at an early age are more likely to stick with them into adulthood. The question is, are the habits they're acquiring going to be serving them well, or not? Impeccable manners are a habit that, if learned, will pay dividends throughout their lives, as well as enhance your relationship with them.

You're welcome!

Reflection and Discussion Questions:

1. Become more aware of your own manners. Which can you improve that will be in line with how you want your kids to behave, and will set a good example?
2. Which manners do think are most needed—in society and in your family—based on your current thinking?

Action Steps:

1. Spend a few days observing your kids' manners both at home and when out in public.
2. Identify those manners that could be improved upon and discuss with your kids why they are important.

WRITE LOVE LETTERS

Words of encouragement and recognition you offer to your kids make a difference. But they're not permanent. Dennis Trittin, author of *Parenting for the Launch* and *What I Wish I Knew at 18*, says, "Raising children is one of the most amazing responsibilities we'll ever be given. We need to be strategic about how we go about doing it. The more we understand that, the more we can come alongside and be a coach and help them understand their uniqueness, their value, how much we believe in them, and how much God believes in them, too.

All of the investments in relationships that we make with our kids—they will pay off. Focus on building a strong relationship, built on trust, and do whatever you can to be their biggest encourager along the way."

One way to positively impact our kids and to create something that's permanent is to write them a love letter. Identify a special day or occasion coming up as an opportunity to present your best thoughts about your child. Maybe you'll decide to do it for each of your children when they reach a certain age. Or, maybe you'll decide to do it every year on your kid's birthdays, marking hallmarks you've noticed in the past year. You'll decide what is best for your family.

What you might do for a son, for example, is write out what you see as his uniqueness, how much you value him, and what value you see he offers to your family, how much you believe in him, what you admire (especially character qualities and decisions that demonstrate his maturing), what you feel the future holds for him, and how much God loves him and believes in him. Then present it to him on that day. Have you ever done this? Can you tell the story? Or do you know someone else who did?

The first time I did this was when I took our oldest son on an outdoor adventure trip. After we had spent several hours together just talking amid the tall timber in the Hansel Adams Wilderness, I then went off by myself with a pad of paper and a pen. For the next hour, I wrote my love letter to him. Included in my letter were my thoughts about why I loved being his father, qualities I admired about him, why I was proud of him, times I'd seen him overcome obstacles, the impact he was having on his siblings as their older brother, apologizing for times I messed up, and my commitment and pledge to always be there for him. I concluded the letter with my blessing for the rest of his life and encouragement and ways to deepen his faith as he continues his faith journey.

In my case, at the end of the evening, while sitting around a glowing campfire, I, along with the other five fathers in our camp, each took turns reading our letter out loud to our child. To say there were a few tears shed, both from the fathers and the kids, would be an understatement.

My example can provide you with a framework, but there's no right or wrong way, so long as you write from your heart and include what will be meaningful to your child. In order to get started, identify an upcoming special event like a birthday or graduation, or just an appropriate date you select. It doesn't need to be in the wilderness or on a special occasion. When you've picked the date, allow ample, uninterrupted time prior to the event to prepare your letter. Many parents are often hesitant to initiate this exercise because they don't feel they're good at writing or doubt they'll have enough to say. If that's you, put those feelings aside and just start. Once the writing process begins, you'll often be surprised by the content that flows.

Expect that it will take more than one sitting to finish your letter. Get started by creating an initial draft. Then set aside what you've written for a day or two to allow your subconscious to keep working, after which you'll have more to add.

I know we all get busy and think we'll always have tomorrow to do this. But, we don't know that. None of us—or our kids—are guaranteed tomorrow. You will never regret taking time to write and share your letters with your kids. And I can promise, over the years, your kids will receive many gifts, cards, certificates, and plaques, most of which will end up being tossed, boxed up, or forgotten about. But your love letter to your kids will become a cherished treasure and one, most likely, they'll keep in their special drawer, within reach, and read many, many times.

Reflection and Discussion Questions:

1. Was a love letter or written affirmations something you received from your dad or mom?

2. If yes, how did they make you feel? If not, how do you think they might have made a difference in your life?

Action Steps:

1. Re-read the quote by Dennis Trittin and seek to fully understand and embrace the rich words that are written.

2. Pick a time and begin creating the document, including the items described above that you'd like to share with your children. On a special occasion, or at a time when you sense your child could use a pick-me-up, present the letter. If distance is a factor, it's suitable to mail the letter. Email is a last resort.

FINAL THOUGHTS

This book is an invitation for you to learn how to fall in love with your kids again and to re-establish a right relationship, if that's been missing. Our children were given to us to enjoy as we guide and journey with them along the road of life. Despite the challenges that will arise, we want joy to be preeminent in our daily interactions with them. Part of that joy is getting to know them and their gifts, talents, and passions.

If you have more than one child, you have most likely witnessed how unique they are from one another. Being a student of our children, so we learn about them and from them, is one of the blessings of being their parent.

Without a doubt, parenthood helps shape us into better human beings, if we approach it with the right mindset. We have a responsibility as their parents to take the role seriously by each day becoming a better parent than we were the day before.

Often when talking to parents who are struggling, I ask them what they've been reading or listening to so they can improve their parenting skills. Usually, all I receive back is a blank stare . . . in other words . . . nothing. They are putting little or no effort into understanding how they could improve. Instead, they are likely to quickly shift the blame to their kids.

Children aren't perfect, nor should we expect perfection from them. And we parents aren't perfect either, so why would we have that expectation? But, we have been given the ability to learn and grow in all aspects of life, including parenting. Most likely, you know people who spend hours and hours working out, perfecting their golf swing, figuring out problems at work, or being entertained . . . but almost no time learning how to become a better parent. And while there's nothing inherently wrong with those activities, it's hard to understand how something so important as parenting could be left to chance or intuition.

The principles presented in this book provide insight for a new way of thinking—a new mindset—especially if you didn't have this type of modeling growing up. Kids, for example, who've been through the foster system often have inconsistent modeling, at best. You may not have been raised in a healthy environment. But that doesn't disqualify you from establishing the kind of experience for your children you wish you had as a kid.

It's probable you'll need to modify and adapt some principles and strategies presented to fit your specific circumstances. They are intended to help you start thinking differently and find common sense solutions to recurring or unique challenges that accompany parenting. It'll be important for your success to be patient with yourself as you work to establish new, improved ways of parenting. The parenting habits we have now didn't just sprout overnight. We've nurtured our methods carefully regardless of whether or not they are serving us or our children well.

Irrespective of where you are in the parenting journey, if there is room for improvement, start today! Looking back with regret at things you know you could have done better doesn't really help. Your past does not have to determine or equal your future. Move forward with optimism and confidence.

If you've really messed up, share that with your children. And let them know you are working to become a better parent. As was admitted, we aren't perfect. Your journey forward will require changes from them and from you. Some they may like and some they may not. Make sure they know with certainty that you are for them, and are working to improve, in order to help them become capable, well-adjusted, productive adults . . . as you strive to establish a more joy-filled home.

The best parenting gift we can give our children is a dad and mom who are committed to each other and who stay married. Additionally, they need to see us growing together as a couple and loving and serving each other. Unfortunately, it's common in today's world for married couples to grow distant, focusing on the needs and activities of the children and their work, instead of each other. Children need to understand, even though they are a top priority in our life, they take a back seat to our relationship with each other as a married couple.

And now a word about prayer. If you are not already, I hope you will become a praying parent. Throughout our kids' development, from the time they can walk until they get married, our children need us to cover them in prayer. Scripture is abounding with directives for us to pray. If prayer were not an essential part of the Christian life, the Bible wouldn't be so consistent in encouraging us to pray. Of course, the nature of our prayers for our children change as they go through the different life stages. And when we're involved in the lives of our children, we'll know what to pray for.

If you are a single parent, there are unique distinctions you'll undoubtedly encounter. Rest assured, the principles presented in this book still very much apply to your situation. In fact, many may be even more vital and foundational as you work to have the most positive influence you can, despite being one parent short.

Be encouraged! You can experience joy and satisfaction (even through the valleys along the way) as you strive to become a better parent. Make joy-filled, purposeful parenting one of your primary goals. As you journey with your children, you can facilitate their growth so they thrive in all dimensions of life: physically, mentally, emotionally, relationally, and spiritually. But don't stop with them. To truly have a positive influence on your children, be committed to maturing and flourishing in each of those life areas *yourself*. Accept the challenge so both you and your children will benefit from parenting practices that will bring out the best in *all* of you!

ABOUT THE AUTHOR

Miles Mettler, PhD is an ambassador for Focus on the Family, a global Christian ministry located in Colorado Springs, Colorado, and dedicated to helping families thrive. Originally from South Dakota, Miles grew up on a farm with his parents and four older brothers. He attended South Dakota State University, where he received his bachelor's and master's degrees.

Afterward, he led the fledgling Brooking Wellness Program for eight years before returning to school, attending Arizona State University to study exercise/wellness and behavior change. Upon receiving his doctoral degree, he served as the general manager of the Mettler Center, LLC, a health/fitness and rehabilitation center in Champaign, Illinois, and then as director of Saint Mary's Wellness Center in Reno, Nevada.

A lifelong learner, Miles is certified as a life coach, a Leading from Your Strengths facilitator, and self-talk trainer. He enjoys speaking, coaching, writing, and opining on his blog at MilesMettler.com. He and his wife, Christy, have four children: one in high school, one in college, one in the US Air Force, and one working as a writer.

A Family Vision Statement

This is an example of our family's vision statement (Principle 2).

Family Plan

Overall Vision: To live a life, raise a family, engage in work, and serve others in a manner that glorifies God every day in every way.

Area Visions:

1. **Home:** Our home is a sanctuary where each family member always feels secure and safe and welcomed and loved in all situations. Grounded in God's unconditional love, we are a dynamic unit, in which unconditional love for each other is openly demonstrated through acts of love, kindness, patience, and forgiveness. Our home is filled with joy and laughter and music and with positive emotion and energy that is reflected in the attitudes each of us display. It is a place dedicated to creating lasting memories based on daily experiences and established family traditions. Our home is open and inviting to family and

friends who are inspired by what they witness. Our home functions effectively because everyone looks for ways to serve each other and contributes to the daily duties with a spirit of joy and gratitude. Finally, our home is filled with thanksgiving for what God has blessed and entrusted us with during our time on earth.

Key Words: sanctuary, safe, joy, laughter, love, patience, serve, gratitude, thanks

2.   **Marriage:** Our marriage is a unification based on trust and of service to each other. We are soul mates and best friends, open with each other and willing to be vulnerable in each other's company. There is no one's company we'd rather be in. We are each other's best cheerleaders, and encouragers in everything honorable we do. We openly show each other affection, never distant or leaving for granted how much love we have for each other. We seek to understand each other's desires and needs and to willingly support what those are. Our marriage is openly witnessed by our children and serves as an example and model for what we aspire their marriages to be like. Finally, we are committed fully to each other, acknowledging that it was God who brought us together and we are dedicated to honoring and glorifying Him in the way we treat, respect, admire, support, encourage, forgive, and love one another.

Key Words: unification, trust, loving, faithful, kind

3.   **Children:** Our children are treasures, each perfectly made the way God intended, entrusted to us to care for, nurture, and cherish. They each have their own gifts, talents, traits, and personalities, which are understood and appreciated and nurtured. Most impor-

tantly, each child knows Jesus and has an intimate relationship with Him, understanding who He is and how much He desires to know each of them. Each is secure in God's love and it is that security that enables them to be confident in themselves. Each is a leader in their life journey, which emanates all things that are worthy and just and honorable. Each of their lives is filled with joy and peace because of the choices they make and the obedient lives they willingly live, knowing that their reward comes in eternity.

Key Words: treasure, inspire, encourage, hope, compassion, obedient

4. **Faith:** Our faith is our rock, grounded in God's unconditional love, on which our foundation as a family is embedded. As a family, we are growing daily in our faith and in our relationship with our Lord and Savior. Attending church is a highlight of our week, as are our family devotionals and times of sharing. We acknowledge that God hates sin and so we strive to lead and live a life like Jesus. We are prepared for good times and bad times that will befall our family and know that through all situations, good and bad, our faith is unwavering. We hold each other accountable to the standards that God created, guarding against the temptations of the earthly world. We are cognizant, as a family of faith, that the Evil One is lurking, tempting, and testing, seeking to unravel our faith in the Lord and our commitment to one another. But, like Job, we will withstand all trials and praise and glorify the Lord, trusting in His promise and in His purpose for our lives. Finally, our faith is embedded in the promise of Jesus Christ knowing that this life on earth is preparation for our eternal life. Our trust lies in knowing that Jesus is our Savior and that through Him we are forgiven of our sins and will live eternally with God.

Key Words: rock, foundation, faithful

5. **Financial**: Every financial blessing we receive is given to us as a gift from God, our provider. We have figured out how to add value to this world and have been rewarded financially in return. Acknowledging this, we are faithful stewards of His blessings and commit to returning a portion of our treasure for His glory and to expand His kingdom. We are thankful for all that we have, knowing that He knows our needs and provides accordingly. We know that the more we are blessed the more is expected of us and gratefully accept that honor and obligation. No matter how much we receive, we are humble servants and stewards always grateful, never prideful, but fully accept the gifts we have knowing that it is God's will to enjoy our time on this earth and use this time in preparation for what is to come.

Key Words: blessing, servants, generosity, giving, thankfulness, stewardship

6. **Work:** Our work is a service dedicated to using our time and talents to glorify God. We passionately engage in work that is filled with a transcendent purpose and service. Fully dedicated to what we do, we joyfully support each other in our labor knowing that each day we become closer to fulfilling the true purpose to which God calls us. Having established that God, family, and work, respectively, are our priorities, we manage our time and responsibilities striving to achieve balance, acknowledging that sacrifice will be needed in each area. We look forward to the day of reckoning when we are held accountable and long to hear the words, "Well done, good and faithful servant."

Key Words: service, passion, purpose, support

7. **Lifestyle:** Our lifestyle is one of worship. Our lives are a tribute to the sacrifice that Jesus paid on the cross. We seek to honor Him in all ways by the choices we make and the things we do. Our lives are filled with meaningful activity anchored by the care and dedication we take of ourselves through good nutrition and regular exercise. We see life as an experience and take pleasure in creating experiences and adventures that surround us in the beauty and wonder of God's creation. We enjoy doing activities as a family, including recreational sports, games, and hobbies. We also support and encourage each other in pursuit of individual interests that are expressions of our talents, gifts, and passions. We base all our decisions, especially those that impact the family, on the leading of God through prayer.

Key Words: tribute, honor, peace, self-control, goodness

APPENDIX TWO

DEVELOPING ACCOUNTABILITY

Everyone benefits from accountability. To help develop accountability with our children, as well as facilitate their growth and maturity, it's best to have a simple system assuring we can be consistent. The system should achieve accountability, without conjuring up feelings like they're in school again.

Pick a time when the mood is right for having a self-reflective conversation with your daughter, for example. (This works equally well with sons, of course.)

1. Lay the foundation by explaining your intent to help her to grow and mature. In addition, use this time to discuss the goals she has for herself. You want to partner with her to grow as a young lady and become the person she aspires to be.
2. Identify "To Be" Goals:
    a. <u>Pre-teen years</u>: Ask her to identify up to five character qualities she feels are important. It's possible they will include areas in which she recognizes she struggles. To help stimulate thinking, ask her what characteristics or qualities she

admires in some of her friends or people she knows. Examples likely to surface include traits like dependable, honest, generous, forgiving, patient, kind, happy, etc. Have her write down her top five To Be Goals.

b. <u>For teens</u>: In addition to the suggestions mentioned above for pre-teens, ask her to identify character qualities she'd like her kids to have when she's a mom. What this will reveal are the traits that are most important to her and, most likely, what she aspires to exemplify, as well. Have her write down her top five To Be Goals. Since kids are sponges and mirrors, discuss how important it is for her to model those same qualities.

3. Identify "To Do" Goals: In addition to establishing your child's To Be Goals, also discuss and write down her To Do Goals. Depending on the age of your child, it'll include things like picking up toys, keeping room clean, doing homework, practicing piano for 20 minutes, exercising for 30 minutes, drinking six glasses of water, reading one chapter in her Bible a day, etc.

4. To help guide the discussion, identify a few items that fall under each of these categories: Talents/Skills to Develop, Health-Related, Faith/Devotional, Education/Personal Development, Activities/Hobbies, Connection/Service, and Contribution/Chores/Financial.

5. On a piece of paper, or with a Word document or Excel spreadsheet, make up the list of To Be Goals followed by the To Do Goals. At the end of each day, take five minutes with your child to review the list and have her rank on a scale from 1 (poor) to 10 (best) how she thinks she did.

6. For each of the items, focus first on what she did well. Unless the number was 1, there will be something she did or an example she can give; second, what's one thing she can do better for

each category (unless it was a 10—then discuss how to repeat or continue doing it).

This exercise is best done in a positive, forward-looking manner. It's not a time to condemn, in any fashion, shortcomings your child may have had that day or week. Remember, you're their partners in this exercise.

If you have teenagers, instead of you being their accountability partner, they could be that for each other. Or, they could have a trusted friend, who has their best interest at heart, be their accountability partner by having a five-minute phone call each night. (If each night seems too ambitious or not realistic, start with once a week. But keep in mind, daily will yield better and quicker changes.)

Implementing this process will help establish a system of accountability for the rest of their life. We are not meant to go through life alone, and we all need the assistance of others to become our best selves. By practicing this at an early age, your kids are much more likely to belong to a life group or have other methods of accountability as they go through adulthood. They'll have experienced the benefits and understand how valuable this practice is for their growth and success.

As the saying goes, "When you're inside the bottle, you can't read what's on the label." The quote emphasizes the value of having someone you trust provide you with regular feedback and accountability. It's why there are life coaches and health coaches and performance coaches and business coaches who help people become better than they could be on their own.

If you want the best for your kids, offer the gift of being their encourager and coach as their accountability partner. It starts by helping them identify their unique To Be and To Do goals.

Recommended Reading

1. *The Men's Study Bible*, NLT
2. *Have a New Kid by Friday* by Kevin Leman
3. *Instant Influence* by Michael Pantalon
4. *Shame Lifter* by Marilyn Hontz
5. *The 12-Week Year* by Biran Moran and Michael Lennington
6. *The Five Dysfunctions of a Team* by Patrick Lencioni
7. *The Five Love Languages* by Gary Chapman
8. *The Happiness Advantage* by Shawn Achor
9. *The One Minute Manager* by Ken Blanchard
10. *The 7 Habits of Highly Successful People* by Stephen Covey
11. *The Success Principles* by Jack Canfield

A free ebook edition is available with the purchase of this book.

To claim your free ebook edition:

1. Visit MorganJamesBOGO.com
2. Sign your name CLEARLY in the space
3. Complete the form and submit a photo of the entire copyright page
4. You or your friend can download the ebook to your preferred device

A **FREE** ebook edition is available for you or a friend with the purchase of this print book.

CLEARLY SIGN YOUR NAME ABOVE

Instructions to claim your free ebook edition:
1. Visit MorganJamesBOGO.com
2. Sign your name CLEARLY in the space above
3. Complete the form and submit a photo of this entire page
4. You or your friend can download the ebook to your preferred device

Print & Digital Together Forever.

Snap a photo

Free ebook

Read anywhere

9 781631 956867